# The National Poetry Review
## Issue Number Twelve

Editor:
C. J. Sage

Assistant Editors:
Ashley Capps
Jill Alexander Essbaum

Contributing Editor:
T. R. Hummer

Book Reviews Editor:
Douglas Basford

## Subscriptions:

Individuals: $15 per year
Institutions: $25 per year
(Please add $6 for subscriptions outside the United States)

Address **subscriptions** to:

Subscriptions
*The National Poetry Review*
Post Office Box 2080
Aptos, California 95001-2080

**TNPR reads magazine submissions in email only.
Please see website for the latest guidelines and reading periods.**

For prize offerings and detailed submission guidelines, please visit
**www.nationalpoetryreview.com**

*The National Poetry Review* is distributed in the United States and Canada by Ingram Periodicals, and indexed by *Humanities International Complete* and *The Index to American Periodical Verse*.

The National Poetry Review Copyright 2003, 2004, 2005, 2006, 2007, 2008, 2009. 2010, 2011, 2012, 2013
All rights reserved
ISBN 978-1-935716-22-8
ISSN 1543-3455

**Cover Art:**
*Show Me A Sign*
Alexandra Eldridge, mixed media
www.alexandraeldridge.com

# Contents

## Poetry

| | |
|---|---|
| Emily Wolahan  *Embleton Bay* | 5 |
| Aaron Anstett  *Care and Feeding* | 8 |
| Maggie Smith  *Deer Field* | 10 |
| R. T. Smith  *Revenant* | 12 |
| Tony Trigilio  *Burial* | 14 |
| Les Gottesman  *Rat on a Leash* | 15 |
| Alice B. Fogel  *Variation 16: Actor* | 16 |
| Lynne Potts  *Four poems on Helen Torr and Arthur Dove* | 18 |
| Jadyn DeWald  *Epilogue* | 20 |
| Elizabeth Hughey  *Land Lines* | 24 |

## Book Reviews: 31

Douglas Basford on Mary Ann Samyn's *The Boom of a Small Cannon*

Dorine Jennette on Emily Rosko's *Prop Rockery*

Gerry LaFemina on Claire Bateman's *Cronology*

## Essay: 43

Erika Lutzner and Douglas Basford  *One hears repeatedly, the role of elegy is:*

Elizabeth McLagan  *Smoke of Labor, Fog of Uncertainty*

## About the Contributors: 55

Emily Wolahan

## *Embleton Bay*

This incredible wager of better

sets off the campaign; its brightness burns

out the edges, splits itself as long tracks

of seawater finger the beach, then unite.

The vacation homes on the bluff

spread their empty approach over rain,

severing clouds.

                      Often the size of things

confuses me. Some appear hideous,

engorged like painted balloons,

their faces stretched so far the colors

pale. We find ourselves standing

on dank sand, sinking and silent. How old

it all looks. The light somehow abandoned

post-apocalypse. The architectural features

bred between wars.

                              I will climb inside

the bristles of that bare bright hedge

and winter until a swimming-pool-blue

horizon.

                              Then I'll unpack.

Some kelp has clumped on the sand,

the moat around it deepening as the sea

retreats. Tendrils fanned, its glisten

bodily and internal. We can try.

And the payoff increases and the loss.

We follow a path into the dune grass—

Oh, motley solutions, tools, promises:

you are holding back the sea.

Aaron Anstett

## *Care and Feeding*

Some number what—10,000 scintilla?—swing
like saloon doors, invisibly hinged, upon

and in this heat-blurred landscaped and who-poured ocean:
underwater flower corral, nosed about by monsters.

On land, many piñatas my brain-shaped
sway, one for each cell left,

and as blindfolded batters gather, I forget
which firework my soul most longs for, hearing

disembodied conversation through wallboards,
but, good start, air condensed to water sweating down milk glass

as elsewhere cows' stomachs translate grasses,
and I greet the day as so often it is: as-is,

each wee hour dream my new career: obit punch-up,
collective noun creation: squalor of Anstetts,

bickering of in-laws, or assign myself such perilous missions
as searching glove boxes, trunks in impound lots for what-all's

whereabouts and attendant engineering specs

to nth-level granularity and zoom-in view

and the vanishing point toward which, on what so-and-so's say-so, the 10,000 things drift.

Maggie Smith

## *Deer Field*

My daughter wants to know where the deer are.
We used to see them across the street

from the airport's long-term parking lots,
before backhoes tore down the trees

and piled them in the grass.
At the intersection of Broad and James,

I tell her all of this was forest
before she was born, and it was full of deer,

but they had to leave when people came
and cleared the land for buildings—

that gas station, that drug store—
and roads, like the one we're on now.

Even where our house stands once
was wilderness. She says it makes her sad.

The few bare trees left are leafed
with black birds, wings trembling

a little in the wind. The sky is a single sheet

of corrugated cloud—rippled but seamless

as if to prove it was not manufactured.
She doesn't ask what they are building

by the airport, in what we called Deer Field.
It doesn't matter. I have changed her.

I have given her the first in a long list
of disappointments, clearing away a perfect,

wild space in her to make room for it.

R. T. Smith

*Revenant*

The head, aggressive in profile,

eye still tinted like a cinder,

the rest of the horse is fading

into drab clay the color

of mist when the shard flashed

in a sunshaft that morning

I was walking the field

following the voice of a wren.

The mane is flying,

haunches almost invisible,

though the tassel of tail

survives. A slight curve says

this is remnant of a vessel,

the edges slate-sharp, all

summoned from dust and water,

the whirl of the wheel,

then glazed to trap it, forever

still. After decades in exile,

it finds my eye and hand.

Do I love most its heft

or the deft slashes that say

"horse" or perhaps the fact

that I can be this haughty

and feel the arc of his spine

all wind-driven, blood-running

and deathless somewhere

in the arc of my spine?

Also, at its birth, the snarling

horse ran out of a fire.

Tony Trigilio

## Burial

My hands tensed the heavy maple
handle and we tried again.
I scooped the possum
into the palm of my neighbor's
barn shovel. He gave himself up.
His heave of fur defied us —
just enough quiver to tumble
off the shovel.

Blood dried in puffs along his tail.
Moonstruck dull, mouth cut into
a triangle. Eyes black as scabs.
The neighbor pushed him
with a garbage can lid
back onto the shovel. His cracked
smile — like he just botched
a punch line but if he waited a few
more beats we might get it. We walked
delicately, like Haz Mat workers,
to the grass strip between our buildings.
He flexed a claw and it shivered.
He gripped the blade of the shovel.

## Rat on a Leash

The apocalypse of money approaches the spiral of rest.
Someone's got to scatter my ocean of ashes.

Elsewise the crying winter bomblet
and coastal fog of nature's psychobabble
spell out to the congress of murder how
starved people waste gravity, and

someone's got to step forward
in a jacket and tie
the introduction of blame to blame
and right the wrongs and bring the head home.

Old Man Tigris, someone's
the rat on solid quicksand, where to doubt is to drop,
better slowly winding
on a spool on a hill.

## Variation 16: Actor

So. Call me obtuse, it isn't what you think. My angle
on method? It's not some avoidance tactic softshoe

get-me-out-of-*me* shuffle, ta-ta
I'm off to transcend. No, it's a hallelujah

chorus raising the rafters in the theatre
of souls that passes as my skull. Wait up, MacDuff,

attention must be paid. *That's* why I do it—to let each
make a scene center-stage, because *personality*,

you know, is death-defying, that's right, it's all an act
in the wings, and I am as many I's as Zeus

gave Argus and honey, I strut them
like a peacock, in top form. Call me a dodo, I am *not*

extinct when like a bird I fly the coop of earthly bounds,
equity transmigration, toasting a born again role.

I take a fresh soul home with each new script,
and honey, I *can* go home again.

And again and again.  What you see
is not who I *am*.  In my one


singular sensational shape I don and slough a slew
of disparate selves.  Think it's distraction I'm after, anything but


humble little me?  Don't you just wish
*you* could live once in this be-costumed bod, and die


night after night, and die, and die, and die, and still—wonders—*be*
this attractive?  Call me vain.  Shameless.  I'm saving face-


lifts by means of masks.  An I for an I?  Sleight of hand?
Out of body experience?  Honey, it's all here in my vita.


Call me a condiment, in solid standing,
fluid when handled and poured.  Over-


soul, when called I come:  It's sexy but not
sexual, lovely but hardly love, escapade, yes,


but never escape.  All entrancing and never having
to bow out.  So call me any time.  Any one.

# Lynne Potts

## *Gull with Telephone Wire*

She painted a boat on the flat of the harbor,

filled it with box-houses and set it afloat.

It was their arc for painting, they said

At first they painted together, then he went past.

A gull will take to a telephone wire,

lose itself at sea, then find a stick for a nest.

She had come to the houseboat to paint.

Soon he was Noah; she, whatever is a wife.

## *Smell of Yeast Bread*

*Man came looking for work. When I asked what kind —
he said; I'm a parachute jumper.*
Helen's Diary Entry

When he came to the farm that time urgent

he told her he wanted help;

she was in yarrow with a swap-shop basket

cutting stems with a pair of pinking sheers.

*Surprise* he said, as if he had dropped the sky

she, the smell of yeast bread rising.

When she thought of it years later

it was mostly the yarrow she remembered.

Some thought it a cultivated flower.

She knew it to be wild.

## *Potted Plant**

Market heliotrope succulent meaning sucking the life of.

Period. No children. If you carried one, would it bloom?

Laburnum the other flower, every part poison, even a swallowed

 drop left in a milk-glass vase. Would she do one or the other?

Here's how to paint a house plant: shade it mud to maroon

leave the stem chartreuse and put it in a brown pot.

Would a calibration of child-shadow make an undulation,

incantation for the small *unmentioned*? No one asked.

She was drifting to a vague purple laburnum, absinthe green

in a distinctly absent way.

*Title of a crayon on paper work by Torr, undated.

## *Helen Torr and Arthur Dove: Part 2*

Last day before winter arrived covering
yard bushes with gauze: that was ritual.
A crab's scuttle was something else —
an instinct she knew well. Well, that's how
one learns to survive a shell: protect yourself,
repeat the motion until it's habit
slowly, slowly the outline becomes
apparent — covered feeling, never recovered.

\*

When he couldn't recover from pneumonia,
she had carried tea trays, pallet, paint —
framed his work in the hallway with faint light.
Some days sea and air were the same color
though she no longer called them by name.
She had lived her work by another hand
and that had been that.

Jadyn DeWald

*Epilogue*

I lie
  sleepless

for a few
  minutes—

then return
  to my wife

washing
  my face

in a huge pail
  of water,

on which
  the red moon

sparkles
  down her

white
  forearms.

But I know

    I am sleeping—

I can hear,
   outside

my tent,
   the white-

tailed fawn
   rolling

my ripe
   cantaloupe,

with her
   black muzzle,

toward her
   warm place

in the leaves
   and needles.

Elizabeth Hughey

*Land Lines*

It is a morning after.

It is a next day

and I am godly

standing in my doorway

looking down at the water,

which is held down

by the mist.

Then the clouds

are dragged away

in tiny pieces

like sugar mounds

by insects. The dumb

blue sky, the clear

dumb lake.

Trilling begins,

but the birds aren't

telling us a thing.

I feel smarter

than the stick pines

for knowing at least

something, that yesterday,

the boy was pulled out of

the water, and then stood

on his pale, fat legs and cried.

I am thinking of bridges

and how the view

doesn't try, the mountains

roll over like caged lions,

the sails in the bay, sharp claws

ripping the air. I'm thinking

of what I know and now

it seems like not much,

but still more than the stupid

sand with orphan roots.

I like it in movies

when soldiers run

through rose gardens

and crash into tables

of sherry glasses,

boots clomping mud

through marble hallways.

I like when bombs shatter

stained glass windows

while a man covers

a woman under the raining

shards, in movies. And when

the quarterback falls

out of bounds, knocking

over the camera man,

and the two must be pulled

from their embrace.

I have not yet been pulled

from an embrace

but I have felt the love

of gravity on my back,

like the sun that I am

turning away from

turning back indoors

toward a blue screen

where the ending

is known, at least by

someone, a group

of men and women

in office chairs around

a black oval table,

craning necks to see

the white board

with three possible

endings. Narrowed

down to two, then one:

The driver swerves

the boat into a soft,

sandy bank.

It's a comedy, now.

The wedding party

is thrown overboard in

suits and silks. A groom

dumps a trout

out of his top hat.

The captain wrings

out his notes. The couple

kisses, ankle-deep in water.

I am not thinking about

the couple, though. I am

thinking about the fish

pulsing his gills at the bottom

of the studio pool, chased

and lifted by the green

net and dropped back

into the familiar waters

of his tank, and the tank

covered and secured

in the back of the handler's

van, driving west toward

a garage apartment on the coast,

sloshing and bumping the edges

of the glass with his blushing,

bright mottled body.

# Book Reviews

Mary Ann Samyn, *The Boom of a Small Cannon*
Dancing Girl Press, 2010, 25pp, $7.00
Reviewed by Douglas Basford

    A month ago, my wife and I stopped in an antique store in a small town in western New York and she fell in love with a daffy little framed print, a bit clumsy in execution, of a slightly baffled-looking young woman in a nineteenth-century dress holding a laurel wreath and a slim book. The caption reads, "It is not sufficient to carry off the prize, but we should merit it." Mary Ann Samyn is worthy of honors for her efforts but not so fatally sincere as to avoid saying in her new chapbook *The Boom of a Small Cannon*, as though chapbooks still can't get enough love, "I won blue ribbons for my efforts." There's snark, and then there's snark. Samyn has a wry wit, but despite her bold strokes and lyric leaping, she has the sensitivity in a line like this to hint at questions that matter: What is it we prize? What is it we reward, and how?

    Ordinarily, to find what's worth noting, you have to thresh the grain and winnow out the chaff, the dreck, the dull. This conventional compositional mode, as contemporary poets are fond of saying they have discovered, denigrates the truly unexpected and the quotidian while privileging the overworn luminous. So when Samyn declares, "Everything worked in the regular way / and in the profoundest way," it can be easy to miss her subtle intent. It is not merely that whatever you look at will have a profundity, as she would have had to say blandly, "Everything was ordinary / and profound," but also the estranging weirdness of the "regular way" is only to be understood as things "work," inasmuch as we can *inhabit and participate* in the duality's humming, haunting movement. As much as possible, Samyn enters that space, more lightly and sardonically, though, than does Stevens with his mind of winter: the apt title "Takes One to Know One" doubles as serious ethical concern and the echo of childish taunting, and the poem itself begins with a paradox that makes the old everyday both understandable and impossible: "Speechlessness was old hat." Elsewhere, she writes, "*Admire yourself naked*, the books advise. // But I had already done that." Those lines come from "It's a Dial, Not a Switch," a title which implies that nothing's binary or black and white, that somehow even our environment is relative and manipulatible. Failing that, we can yearn for someplace unnamed, unspecified: "I was ready to move there. I'm almost always ready to move there."

But all this playful philosophizing about the inhabited place to the point of it feeling like one has been there an eternity and nothing is surprising (or is it?—take this "exchange": "I paint for humans, said Rothko. / *Me* too, said Mary Ann." The mockery of Rothko's high seriousness nevertheless has in it the vocalized burst of a genuine delight, "Me too!") has at its origin moments of emotional disequilibrium, a lump in the throat, as Frost called it, and that anchors these poems in an authenticity that permits the fanciful leaps and swerves. The line "What didn't bother me then bothers me now" hovers isolated, double-spaced, like most of the lines do in this chapbook, gathering about it the full impact of its commonsensical abstraction, inviting us to linger on what now burrows under our skin that (perhaps) should have done so years ago. Samyn follows, however, with an equally informal admission: "I'd have thought progress was the reverse."

But progress is not so easy to identify, much as we might desire it mightily, if for no other reason than finding the point of departure, or at least an earlier state of being, is more complicated than our minds will admit. Samyn initiates her sequence with a splash that suggests an inattention preceded this moment, our own, but she jokes enough about it to let us somewhat off the hook: a one-liner with the title, "Now That You've Got My Attention," runs simply, "Start the volcano again; I'm watching." I'm watching *this time* is what she means.

Now that she has your attention, Samyn sounds the title poem, which runs in its entirety like this, minus one line:

> I am equal to the courage of the world.
> 
> I am equal to the world.
> 
> These are the horizontal mysteries, a glacial pace.
> 
> Drastic measures do not stay with the symptom.
> 
> I stay with the symptom.

> *Sunday, Sunday, Sunday—*
> Beauty makes this resounding in me.

I am continually struck by the calm insistence, the boldness of voice, the sense of the geological speed of any changes that occur. The mention of recursiveness in the context of "glacial pace" brings me to retroactively revise what might have been a false impression of Samyn's vaulting imagination: read at the speed we usually read a poem, the "leaps" suggest pistons going at all speed, whereas she is suggesting instead that the grounding is really a form of deep time, of following the very material of the world along its trajectory from what we cannot know to what we cannot know.  In this geographical sense, there is an echo of Bishop's elegy for Lowell— "revise, revise, revise"—as she imagines nature's compulsion to revisit itself. But we cannot ignore the arbitrariness of *"Sunday, Sunday, Sunday,"* its phonetic ambiguity (sundae-Sunday), its echoing of the caricatured voice of a radio advertisement for a monster-truck rally. Nothing can work only in the regular way. Beauty of a sort we cannot *but* anticipate will strike those deep chords, resounding. The line I left out is actually the first, "Engine room of the *trying not to vacate.*"—that "resounding," as of a cannon, overtakes us as the fullness, the often oppressive fullness, of a sound, from which we should do everything in our power not to escape from, and let it gradually subside into echoing repetition and gradual diminishment.

Emily Rosko, *Prop Rockery*
The University of Akron Press, 2012, 77pp, $14.95 paper
Reviewed by Dorine Jennette

        Emily Rosko's *Prop Rockery* invites the reader to a strange, even estranging, yet pleasing feast for the ears, mouth, and mind. Within intriguingly titled pieces like "Stuffed and Strung Up for the Birds," "And So It Was Done Riding the Horse Backward," "King of the Boars," and Shakespearean borrowings like "[If they would yield us but the superfluity while it were wholesome]," Rosko swirls the tactics of collage into the narrative, lyric, and meditative modes. In so doing, she creates poems that are tightly crafted yet wildly unstable layer cakes: of texts, situations, chronologies, narratives, moods, agendas, emotions, and characters.

        Rosko's layer cakes take collage, in which disparate elements contribute to cross- or multiple purposes, and stir it into other modes whereby united elements (albeit sometimes united by associative drift alone) pull in harness together. Rosko's mode-mixing is a contradictory recipe, and *Prop Rockery* is steeped in the delights of the paradoxical. For further flavors of complication, Rosko seeds her lines with complex puns, allusions, and etymological games. She layers her diction, dredging the English language for the shiny bits that rise up through the last five-hundred years, from Shakespeare's plays to now.

        A representative example is "[Accoutred as I was I plungèd in]." The title comes from Shakespeare's *Julius Caesar*, from a passage in which Cassius complains to Brutus that, in essence, Caesar is not so great: Cassius remembers a winter day when he and Caesar leaped into the Tiber river on a dare, trying to swim its width—and it was Caesar who tired and had to be carried to shore by Cassius, not the other way around. Rosko's poem, likewise, narrates the speaker's kvetching against some intimate party in her life. Rosko's poem begins:

        Slippery slope of affects. I wetted
        the words, armed to the teeth.
        I bled first from the eye, then from
        my small heart down. (17)

From these opening lines on, the associations pile up faster than the reader can track them, as Rosko's piece narrates a contemporary relational conflict in the language of an archaic physical and political challenge. Her "slippery slope" conjures up the physically slippery shores of the Tiber river from the *Julius Caesar* passage, and also, appropriately, "slippery slope" in the rhetorical sense of a moral or logical slippery slope. Rosko's slippery slope is of "affects," of emotions and of their facial and vocal manifestations; the affective conflict gets underway with "I bled first from the eye, then from // my small heart down" (17). This weirdly affecting bit sets a new piece of the reference collage in place, as the archaic construction "my small heart down" reminds the reader of the medieval love lyric "O Western Wind" with its "the small rain down can rain," which suggests that the party Rosko's speaker rails against is a lover.

Thus, with Rosko's poem just four lines in, she has already conjured echoes of multiple favorite pieces from ye-olde-English-literature canon, and is positing the Roman power struggle against Caesar as an analog for the relational distress of the speaker, who is getting ready for "a going-at-it / with the right dagger" (17). The fight doesn't go well for the speaker, as things don't go well in *Julius Caesar*: the poem ends, "I ran myself through" (17).

Rosko does brave new things with old figures, as well as old lines. Take, for example, Rosko's paired apostrophes to the sun and moon, "Solar Complaint" and "Lunar Complaint." "Lunar Complaint" begins: "Moon, you are a button-hole anus! Moon, you plagiarize / the sun!" (53). This poem's opening would startle anywhere, but is especially startling as the sequel to the courtly "Solar Complaint." To go from "'why dost thou thus'" (52) at the close of "Solar Complaint" directly to "button-hole anus" on the next page is disconcerting, to say the least. Poems such as "Lunar Complaint" begin in the familiar—in this case, an address to the moon—then swerve wildly, the acute angle of the swerve palpable precisely because we thought we knew, for just a moment, where the poet was going. In "Lunar Complaint" and like pieces, Rosko assembles one poem out of disparate vocal tones, from the waggish "Oh, to be cheese!" to the poem's parting, straight-faced, disappointed "You are not the thing to match or the eye to become" (53).

A key piece in the collection is "Mare's Nest," which

sets an epigraph from Austrian writer Karl Kraus (more on this momentarily) to hover over lines from Denise Levertov, Emily Dickinson, and William Shakespeare, as well as a thirteenth-century nursery rhyme, US environmental law, and a mustang roundup. The poem is loosely organized as a narrative of the roundup, including many a tangent. The poet's sense of play is given full rein: "They had helicopters and GPS, all that / cowboy whoopi ti yi yo" (22). However, in spite of the poem's linguistic buoyancy, the overall mood is one of sadness: "I duke me up, I talk West. Lost / my partner, what'll I do?" (22). Foremost, there is the sadness of the roundup itself, as the horses are "Mowed . . . down with tranquilizers (thump)" (22). There is also the over-layer of sadness created by the speaker's inability to help the horses: in all her roles, throughout her tangents, the speaker is ever an observer, and rather lost, at that. She says, in an apparent state of shock: "So then went the cleaving, the horses / in a stall for study. I looked at and at" (23). This speaker is astute, but helpless, overwhelmed or inundated by the speed and density of her own observation:

> I got to play scout, the ding-dong
> bell-ringer. I took the binocs, the hook,
> a lucky shoe. Had my watch in the radio
> steel tower; got owl-crossed, got assed
> fast, pulled a switcheroo. The whole charade's
> been arranged as presented: the cow
> pies, the triad, the blank afternoon. (22)

The poem's title, "Mare's Nest," is a centuries-old expression that can mean "a hoax or fraud" and/or "an extraordinarily complicated situation" (75). The poem certainly is the latter. During the roundup, the speaker seems to feel herself participating in both a fraud and a complex situation. Underneath her flamboyant diction runs a despairing sense that the roundup is a trick, as in "whole charade" and "Razor-wire / rigged across the range, set for trip" (22). In addition to its individual physical tricks, the roundup plays one complex, overriding conceptual trick by conflating the live animal with its use as a dead animal: "Honesty's a brute; / the steed's side says MEAT" (22). The speaker's linguistic wandering through the piece may be spurred by the impossibility of speaking such brutality plainly, or by her shocked refusal to do so. Yet it seems likeliest that this speaker's linguistic wandering through "Mare's Nest," her compulsive associative layering of allusions, associations, rhymes, and puns, is driven by the extraordinarily complicated nature of language itself: she is unpacking its buried etymologies, the history hoards riding inside old words and expressions.

This brings us to the poem's epigraph, from Karl Kraus: "The closer the look one takes at a word, the greater the distance from which it looks back" (21). The dizzying effect described by this epigraph is both experienced by and produced by the speaker of "Mare's Nest." For example, the speaker says,

> I was shaken as salt. I was
> as industrial as a drill. Oh pity-poor
> fractured me, brain-way-sided, boring
> through and through, full of ballas and glue. (21).

This passage tumbles the reader through familiar expressions, unfamiliarly realigned ("I was shaken as salt"), in addition to its pointed puns ("boring through and through" following "drill"). The passage layers the familiar and the unfamiliar, the old and the new; it sets words that speak to their near neighbors next to words that reach far away from the page. In passages like this one, some of Rosko's words may point simply, physically, to an object or objects; other words or word-clusters reach sideways toward texts, events, or text-events tangentially related to the piece. Some words refer to simple physical objects *and* simultaneously to multiple texts and events set at various angles to the piece. Thus, Rosko is not only collaging together assorted narratives and allusions, but collaging together assorted strategies of word usage—which is to say she is collaging together assorted poetics. This means that some of her lines have very different ideas than other lines about what a word is and what, if anything, it points to. The destabilizing sensation that this layering of references and word-functions creates, which is especially acute in "Mare's Nest," is a consistent ingredient throughout *Prop Rockery*.

In *Prop Rockery*, such perpetually shifting relationships between the poet and her text, between the text and its referents, and among the text's assorted pieces, contribute to the collage energy that enlivens a collection populated by everything from the musical toy of "Two-Bit Song" ("What more pointed than a trout on a spear?" [56]) to nature lyrics like "Cloudland" ("You must not blame me

/ if I talk to the clouds . . . Dispersive, discursive. I should / be a mediator, / a meditator, a meteor" [43]). Even when the poems are not collages in the temporal sense of moving from subject to subject as they unfold across the page, they tend to be collages in the vertical sense, associations stacking up in the air above the page. To read these poems is an experience of dizzying simultaneity. The pleasure of surfeit is the joy of reading *Prop Rockery*.

Claire Bateman, *Cronology*
Etruscan Press, 2010, pp. 72, $17.95
Reviewed by Gerry LaFemina

Claire Bateman's *Coronology* is an ambitious collection of poems—ambitious with its vision, with its desire to explore the possibilities of consciousness and creativity. The book embarks on this enterprise with the opening poem: "A Brief Introduction to the Universe." This interview poem introduces us to the universe of the book, the universe of Bateman's poetics. This is quantum poetry, dense, complicated, intellectual—sometimes overly intellectual—exploring the realms of poetic possibility, of the creative process of the self and of the imagination. But this isn't *Basho's Narrow Road to the Interior*, in which the journey inward is engaged by a literal journey into the interior of Japan; rather, *Coronology* is a theoretical journey into the interior, one suited for our postmodern times.

As with many theoretical projects, the readers of this book are challenged: we're asked to follow complicated sentences across multiple lines, to track metaphors that shape-shift and evolve, and, often, to accept that these ideas and images are "connected to" nothing. This isn't William Carlos Williams's poetry of "no ideas but in things." This is a poetry of no things without ideas first.

The problem for a poetry of ideas, of philosophy—and I was a philosophy major—is that the ideas themselves often take precedence over the poetry. Because the ideas are dense, following the train of ideas can allow prosody to take a back seat. For instance, in the first section of "Luminal," Bateman writes:

> But isn't light as mysterious as darkness;
> isn't what lifts and reveals
> as profound as that which descends and covers?
> There is a glory of the night
> but there is a glory of the day as well,
> which possesses its own cascades and fathoms,
> though the brighter the light,
> the farther it seems to recede...

Although there are lots of interesting ideas here–the

opening dialectic in particular, which begs us to consider all dialectics, and some clever rhetoric (beginning with the "But-" question creates a conversational tone that engages the reader)—there's not a lot of interesting poetics. The lines break on the natural pause, the music is pretty expected, and I'm so caught up following the dialectic of darkness and light, that the slight repetition of "a glory..." has little punch.

Even when Bateman gives us the unexpected image, as she does in the third section of "Luminal," the prosody is fairly muted:

> When you fold a map, you fold the map's light.
> The map finds this unnerving, and responds
> by distorting its surface, multiplying its creases,
> and swelling to half again its bulk,
> though never in a uniform manner.

Although I appreciate the humor of how, refolding a map, one has a difficult time of it, and I like the surrealistic twist of the map doing something to cause this, overall I wonder "where's the ear" in this poem, what's the logic of the line, of the music?

The fact is Bateman can write some musical lines: In "Intellectual Property" she starts with the image of trucks arriving "with the materials for my Big Idea" (a quirky sensibility that recalls the poems of Jeffrey McDaniel). Later she catalogues those materials:

> the bricks, the stones, the mortar,
> the patio, the entertainment systems, the linoleum,
> the polished oak banisters, the cupolas, the flying
>    buttresses,
> the peacocks, the gargoyles, the moat,
> the sheet lightning, ball lightning, forked lightning,
> the sunken grottoes, the rainforest, the cascades,
> the mezzosopranos, the Visigoths, and the parking
>    garage.

Of course, what makes any catalogue poem interesting is the inventory of items being surprising as well as the relationship to each other sonically. Listen to how the "-ol" in linoleum returns in "cupolas", and transforms in "gargoyles," or to how the repetition of those three "lightning"s forces us to experience three different types of lightning, or how the O sound comes to play in almost every line ("stones," "patio," "oak," "moat," "grottoes" and "mezzosopranos")–that O sound, like a mouth open in wonder.

Bateman is able to maintain the poetic muscularity throughout the poem. Later she writes:

> So later that season,
> when my Big Idea had been publicly refuted
> and the components had been carted away,
> I understood that I could take credit
> for nothing–
> not even the conflagration that consumed
> the evidence of all that construction,
> nor the smaller, fiercer fires that followed....

Sure, the abstractions are a bit much, yet here the "con-" sounds that open many of the words—and the alliteration on the hard K sound that leads to those words—power the sentence onward, and they give way literally and aurally to the F sounds in that last line.

Bateman's language has moments of aural flare to compare with her ability to create an image that is both humorous and surprising, but her prosody exists purely on the level of the sentence, and she breaks her lines time and again in accordance to the syntactical demands of the sentence. Perhaps it is for this reason that I find the prose poems the most successful pieces in this collection, for they allow themselves to rely solely on their own rhythms, without the implied craft choices of line breaks.

This is best illustrated in the title poem, a long, abecedarian prose poem; each of its 26 sections works as an encyclopedic entry–or perhaps a wiki-entry–in a database of "crowns" and crown-related items. In this prose poem the sentence does the work of conductor, maintaining the rhythm, while giving us insight into the many dimensions of the poet's universe. Perhaps nothing sums up Bateman's mission than the K entry:

> Because a poet's vocation is to make everything
> difficult that is easy and vice versa, the knotted
> crown becomes him or her with its convoluted
> cluster of filigreed intertwinings. Anyone near
> the poet must resist the temptation to trace and
> retrace the various loops and turnings in order to
> locate the starting point of any of the designs....

There is no mention of beauty in this statement, no mention of artistry.

In the end, that's my beef with a poetics of ideas: it's not the ideas that bum me out—I think much of poetry engages ideas. It's the lack of focus on the poetry, on connecting the reader and the ideas to the beauty of language. Coleridge told us that "poetry is the best words in the best order." While best is a subjective term, reducing poetry to only this playful image making, this bit of anecdote, this blasé surrealism, while removing from it the possibilities offered by rhetoric and rhythm among other techniques, results in a poetry that sacrifices its heart for the crown on its head.

*Coronology* might be a smart book of poems. They have a lot to say and an interesting worldview. Surely Bateman is a smart thinker in these poems, and they often sparkle with moments of imagistic accuracy and imagistic originality. However, I left the poems feeling neither smarter nor enriched from reading them, and although I often nodded my head at moments in the book, I was reminded, ultimately, as to why I gave up philosophy for poetry in the first place.

## Essays

*One hears repeatedly, the role of elegy is:* On Mary Jo Bang's "Worse"
Erika Lutzner and Douglas Basford

> Mary Jo Bang
> Worse
>
> You are in the zebra crossing,
> Moving into the tornado green morning,
> The shabby irradiation
> Of sunlight seen though the hint
> Of rain about to be. Death is
> A jerky reversal of forward momentum.
> Back into memory. Into a cereal bowl
> On a table decades ago, the color of an orange
> Aspirin for a fever at age four
> That produced a heat-filled forehead hallucination.
> Think of a hive made of glass, all the bees,
> Theoretically at least, describable but not all at once.
> That's my mind and you
> Are doing all the things you ever did all at once.
> There are so many
> Of you. Many more than several. Thirty-seven
> Years of behavior. Nothing terrible
> Has happened as yet except the uneven drone
> Inside is an announcement that there will be something
> Like a sting only much much worse.

Every poem in Mary Jo Bang's fifth collection *Elegy* is an homage to her son, Michael. Some poems are haunting and spare, others throb with emotion. This book doesn't so much detail the son's personal life, nor does it make clear whether the death from a drug overdose was accident or suicide, but instead draws the reader into a mother's love for a son and her grief, always in danger of losing control of the lines within each poem. In the poem "Worse," the catastrophic tension between particulars and wholeness most fearfully threatens to rend and paralyze the grief-stricken speaker. It is a visceral piece, full of remembered moments. It tells us what it's like to love someone who is no longer alive;

it allows us to enter into the world of pain of a mother losing her son while memorializing him in the most gentle and fierce ways.

*You are in the zebra crossing, / moving into the tornado green morning.* In these first two lines, there is a stark conjunction: on the one hand, the Polaroid moment of a pedestrian in a crossing, a place presumably of safety assured by law, good will, a social contract, and luck, and yet—as it is not called a mere crosswalk—zanily zoo-y when taken as a literal phrase, zebras stampeding across a street, and on the other hand, the surreal, David Lynch-like image of the "tornado green morning." (Though the gravity and clear-eyed realism behind these lines is easily apparent, the weirdness also recalls a blurb that Bang wrote for Mac Wellman's *Strange Elegies*: "I know of no one who knows more than Mac Wellman about the interstices between desire and nonsense.") Despite evoking atmosphere effects around the bittersweet parting of parent and child—is this her son as a child crossing the street, leaving the house for school in the morning, his mother watching part-nervous, part-proud through a screen door, watching him move among green branches in blustery winds?—it contains inscribed within its internal rhyme (*torn* and *mourn*) the language of the destruction and loss to come.

*The shabby irradiation / Of sunlight seen through the hint / Of rain about to be, Death is / A jerky reversal of forward momentum. Shabby irradiation?* Sunlight seen through the hint of rain about to be? What does it mean? Like the tornado green morning that presages danger, sunlight through the hint of rain is something that can never be again. Which leads us to the next statement, "Death is/A jerky reversal of forward momentum,/Back into memory." Bang's choice to break the line after "Death is" and to place "A jerky reversal of forward momentum," on the next line with "Back into memory" at first glance seems wrong and clumsy. "Death is" 'wants' to be on the same line with "A jerky reversal of forward momentum." Yet, by being separated, each part of the sentence stands on its own and takes on its own significance. Taken together, the movement is as jerky as death itself. Death jerks us out of this world into another place, as does grief. The odd and seemingly awkward motion actually enacts death itself. "Forward momentum" is an interesting word choice because it suggests, like irradiation in the previous line, that energy is moving back and forth.

*Back into memory. / Into a cereal bowl / On a table decades ago, the color of an orange / aspirin for a fever at age four / That produced a heat-filled forehead hallucination.* We are not merely heading back, at the risk of cliché, into memory—back into time, the momentum rewinding—but *into* a cereal bowl, a fortuitous prepositional slip brought on by the momentum of association. Like the break between "Death is" and "A jerky reversal of forward momentum," the break between "Back into memory" and "Into a cereal bowl" at first seems strange, but in fact the cereal bowl, and not merely the memory of it, is the memory. And though the bowl is also presumably no longer accessible save through memory—"On a table decades ago"—it takes on a startling materiality for the mourning voice and, if Freud and Peter Sacks (who applies his theoretical framework to the elegy) are to be believed, becomes a kind of substitution object for the dead loved one. Bang has thoroughly absorbed the tradition of the English elegy as traced by Sacks, submitting herself to the battery of questions that buffet the mourner, including this one from another poem in the book: "How could I have failed you like this? / The narrator asks // The object." The emotionally distanced "narrator" speaking to the "object" also accords well with both common sense and post-psychoanalytical takes on the psychology of mourning, the "object" being, in fact, the box containing the narrator's son's ashes.

    The cereal bowl is anything but a conventional substitution object or traditional keepsake, marking Bang's "work of mourning" as decidedly contemporary and, dare we say, postmodern. The heavy enjambment and shifting figuration in "The color of an orange / Aspirin for a fever at age four" further unsettle our sense of how consolation can possibly come amid a landscape populated with such mass-produced objects. Not only is the orange a reminder that it is the only color to be an actual object, but it is also a fruit that one might expect to see in a bowl, implying that the bowl is what it contains (and vice versa), a complicated vessel metaphor that will be revisited later in the poem.

    However much the reader might relate to this orange aspirin and be somehow comforted by the inference of maternal attentiveness, a couple of complications arise. First, the aspirin is likely only good for alleviating some of the symptoms of a fever or a "heat-filled forehead hallucination," leading to the aching realization that, as in Marjorie Perloff's discussion of the "collision and collision with History" in Susan Howe's poetry—"What difference a phoneme makes!" she exclaims—there is a short phonetic distance and an unbridgeable semantic-etymological gap between *care* and *cure*. Like the mother of the sick child who cannot *cure* him of his fever but can only *care* for him, so the mother mourning her son cannot *cure* him, and thereby literally bring him back from the dead. She can only *care* for him, a word which in the medieval period meant to sorrow, grieve, or lament, a sense now lost through the winnowing of time. Second, the bowl is the container of a daily victual, ordinary nourishment, whereas its color-based link is to an aspirin, a pharmaceutical product, a drug, a harrowing reminder that the son had died of an overdose. Despite these dark undercurrents and the sense of reeling urgency, the imagery is, nevertheless, like the orange objects themselves, somewhat lulling, aesthetically pleasing in a modern sense, ostensibly practical, and palliative.

  *Think of a hive made of glass, all the bees, / Theoretically at least, describable but not all at once. / That's my mind and you / Are doing all the things you ever did all at once.* A hive made of glass isn't, we assume, penetrable, but the suggestion might be that we can see the inner activity, like the hives set on display in museums and elsewhere for children to watch the dance of bees flush with discovery of a new field of flowers and a desire to describe how to get there—the seamless communication via a limited set of socially accepted signs and signifiers. And yet the hive seems less like it's constrained within two dirty vertical panes, Bang's language instead seeming to suggest something of a swarming within the hive, shaped like a "mind" and less like a solid bell-jar than a Swarovski glass easily shattered. The next line is difficult: "Theoretically at least, describable but not all at once." It's possible to understand it on a visceral level, but difficult to break down. The bees are her discrete memories of the son, and each can be described individually but it doesn't seem possible to create a unified whole that stands for the person who is now gone.

  And yet, that's exactly what happens: "That's my mind and you / Are doing all the things you ever did all at once." By breaking the line between "That's my mind and you" and "Are doing all the things you ever did at once" she is insisting that both of these things are true. This is a very intimate moment in the poem and the intimacy is produced just with a line break. That intimacy, that cohabitation of the one line is the elegiac speaker bringing, as Allen Grossman put it, the absent back into presence, even if the traditional face of the absent beloved is now replaced with an incoherent swarm of memories, the individually "describable" elements yielding what could be termed an "emergent" phenomenon or property, which is what cognitive scientists are proposing the mind is.

*There are so many / Of you. Many more than several. Thirty-seven / Years of behavior.* This continues the conceit of the many-in-one, but the linebreaks toss and twist the subjects in a series of progressive revelations, as it appears that rather than sheer confusion at the numerousness of memory and existence, Bang allows her speaker a modicum of control—she is finding language for it all. But she settles here at the end of this set of lines on "behavior," a word so often used to describe children's actions when they are yet under the control of their parents. But Bang's son was no longer under that regime, an adult nearly twice past being able to legally recognize himself. His behavior, here initially seen in sum, drops suddenly to a single, self-destructive act, itself perhaps the culmination of one thread or several strands of unstoppable behavior, which are of course not truly to be removed from the full fabric.

*Nothing terrible / Has happened as yet except the uneven drone / Inside is an announcement that there will be something / Like a sting only much much worse.* This single sentence is broken many times. It is a death announcement. "Nothing terrible has happened yet except the uneven drone." The droning sound of the bees suggests the coming danger just as the move from the zebra crossing into the tornado green morning did, and yet that sound also feels impotent, trapped inside the glass. As a sound that goes on and on endlessly, it feels as though this will forever be the situation. It can refer to speaking or in music it can refer to tonality. It's used frequently in music as a method of repetition to evoke a certain feeling. It is as though Bang, in a gesture of humility, even self-deprecation, in the face of unrecountable loss, implies that she drones throughout the poem, perhaps even the whole book, rather than what the traditional elegy would have done: *intone*. To intone would be to engage with poetry's ancient role of the causational, the performative language, as J. L. Austin saw it, bringing about what it says should happen. But to drone instead means to make nothing happen, poetry's modern curse.

It is also worth noting that in a hive, the drone, or male bee, has no sting; his sole purpose is to fertilize the queen. He can do no harm and has no power, a mere parasite. He doesn't even feed himself and dies after fertilizing the queen. If the son is the drone in the poem, Bang is too, in a different manner. But there is a sting, or something magnitudes worse, the implication being that something will happen of its own accord, something catastrophic. "Inside there is an announcement that there will be something" stands on a line by itself, an intriguing study of perspective-shifting and vagueness before the final line's blow, draws much of its understated power from the syntactical readjustment caused by the enjambment with the previous line, which causes a sudden lurch forward to the unexpected "announcement," which rather than being delivered from outside is instead found within the narrator's "mind." Much of the poem is built on language that operates on the prospect of something awful soon to happen, but as we have seen the hive metaphor emerges only because the event the poem commemorates has already happened. What remains is the harrowing threat of a mental breakdown, or so it seems. Or we are in a confusing conflation of different points in time such that the sudden blow is something, in a sense, foreseen.

Bang has built the elegy on the suspense of what control can be had by language over circumstance. Poems in her collection after *Elegy* play with the polyassociative in similar ways, hinting that this touch-and-go may hold the key to overlaying language on experience. Even the title, *The Bride of E*, by which she really means "the bride of Experience," a somber phrase indicating our weddedness to what we cannot control, also calls to mind the grotesquely daffy "Bride of Frankenstein," created to satisfy the yearning of another creation. Experience, she implies, is not merely an inhuman force, but a creation of our own. We may be none the wiser for seeing that. Without self-pity, she engenders emotion in "Worse," allowing the reader both to feel her sorrow and wonder about the uses of elegy in our times. This poem, about grief and memory, about what it is to love and to lose the one you love, is successful because it is a tightly woven elegy in which Bang moves the reader into provocation and pain, while never forgetting the focus—her son.

Bibliography

Austin, J. L. *How to Do Things with Words*. 2nd ed. Cambridge: Harvard UP, 1975.

Bang, Mary Jo. *Elegy*. St. Paul, MN: Graywolf, 2007.

----. *The Bride of E*. St. Paul, MN: Graywolf, 2009.

Erickson, Robert. *Sound Structure in Music*. U of California P, 1975.

Grossman, Allen. *The Sighted Singer*. Baltimore, Johns Hopkins UP, 1992.

Perloff, Marjorie. "'Collision or Collusion with History': The Narrative Lyric of Susan Howe." Contemporary Literature 30.4 (Winter 1989): 518-33. <http://www.jstor.org/stable/ 1208613>.

Sacks, Peter. *The English Elegy*. Baltimore: Johns Hopkins UP, 1985.

"Theatres of Eternal Music." Textura (Feb. 2005). <http://www.textura.org/archives/ articles/ dronesarticle.htm>.

Vickery, John. *The Modern Elegiac Temper*. Baton Rouge: Louisiana State UP, 2006.

Wellman, Mac. *Strange Elegies*. New York: Roof Books, 2005.

Winston, Mark, *The Biology of the Honey Bee*. Harvard UP, 1986.

*Smoke of Labor, Fog of Uncertainty:*
An Explication of Nance Van Winckel's "Mister."
Elizabeth McLagan

Mister
Nance Van Winckel

He was what we half expected, bringer
of order to the orchard. Pears by pears, plums
by plums. His mind moves and our bodies stand
and follow. The hoes drag along.

Taking our fear as a given, he'll start a song
at dusk. Merrily, as mirror and echo, we till
and sing. Gone a-rowing. Smoke and fog
on the water, we row we know not where.

In the real river cattle cool off, then step
one by one into starlight. If we reach the last
peach trees, he'll have the lantern lit. On
we go. The hoes' enormous shadows
rise and fall across our small ones.

Smoke fogs the water
and still no shore in the song.

from *No Starling*

(University of Washington Press, 2007)

At first reading the title seems to provoke more questions than information. Who is this? Anonymous male authority, possibly resented; I think "Hey, Mister," something yelled to a stranger. The poem's first sentence, cutting across a line break, continues this reference and establishes the point of view. Something about the half-expectation pulls us further. But we're in an orchard, a known place of pears and plums. The third line introduces a strange mind/body split, and with the additional detail of the hoe, the "we" proposed as a band of workers, the mister our boss. But something feels off, not quite imbued with the dirt of the real world. The tone is dreamlike, the action entirely biddable. Familiar, and yet mysterious: what a great place to be!

The second stanza continues to focus on our unnamed leader, now at dusk and because of our fears, offering comfort. Bringer of order, starter of song. This guy seems like a little god of the orchard, and I am beginning to fall under his spell. The group's response is harmonious: without thinking, following orders. We could be in a Bruegel painting, hoeing the weeds, shouldering our baskets of fruit. What could be the fears we sing of? Will the crop fail? Will there be plenty or starvation? In the dream world of an elemental and ancient ritual of work and play the stanza concludes with an image of rowing. Without a destination but captivated, surrounded by obscuring elements, we are pleasantly lulled and. . . lost. The ending cracks the pleasant bucolic surface of the stanza, and we are left, as at the end of the first stanza, not entirely sure of where the poem is taking us.

The third stanza opens with a dazzling image, well, at least one that I admire, liking as I do to drive along and see cattle grazing in fields, pleased by their beauty and thankful that I don't have to tend them. We've returned to the real world, albeit one lit by stars. We've passed from the dusk of the second stanza to full night. As a child growing up in rural Oregon, I remember waking to the sound and sight of a neighbor plowing his fields, his tractor's single headlight a beacon across the summer field. In the long growing season, the agricultural workday stretches into night and is rarely completed. The conditional in the second line of this stanza implies it's by no means certain we'll get there. The stanza concludes with the return of the simple implement of work, here enlarged. We are made small by fatigue and constant effort.

Each of the three preceding stanzas have alternately lulled and startled the reader, enacting the transaction between expectation and reality, mind and body, fear and song. The concluding couplet recombines the elements with a powerful shock: *still no shore in the song*. I have to admit I fell in love with this poem's last line, and then with the poem. No resting place to be had, at least in the trance state of the song, which is the trance state accompanying work, needing no thought, only action.

The sizzle of the poem's last utterance sends me right back

to the top. I think of this "Mister" as a demi-god, or artisan, one who brings order, but what else that answers the assertion "half-expected"? Since the most unexpected part of the poem is its final assertion of ultimate uncertainty, is our mister the one who brings order, but not certainty? Isn't this often the expectation we have of our leaders, big or small? Well, yes, but so early in the poem I feel the diminishment of this generalization, and attractive as it is, I want to put it aside and return to the literal orchard. Reading through the first stanza again, noting its fruit, instructions, effort, implements, I pause at the second stanza's first line to consider the pairing of "fear" and "song." More than the fear of a failed harvest, the word now seems to embrace any fear that urges us to singing.

The poem moves with a supple energy in medium length sentences that break across the line, alternated with short fragments. In the first two stanzas about half the lines end with words emphasizing action, while the other half of the lines end with nouns. At a key point in the poem, lines 12 and 13 are enjambed more radically, with an adjective and a preposition, emphasizing the relentlessness of the labor here evoked. The poem begins in the past tense with references to the future, and conditional, but mostly exists in a seemingly endless present tense (work sometimes feels like this).

I discover with pleasure the word "merrily," which I had overlooked in the first reading and hear the familiar children's round (row, row, row your boat). I'm also relishing the dance of paired words: mirror and echo, till and sing, smoke and fog, and finally, again, the shoreless song. The language is as simple as bread, and as nourishing.

Elsewhere in *No Starling* are poems that echo the same concerns. In "I am On a Break" a waitress outside smoking on her break tells us "I'd been/dimed and quartered, spit at, /ogled and ignored." In "The Winter Cow" a boy must milk and nurse a cow whose hooves are failing. "He'd tried to sing a few songs for her/ but there wasn't one that didn't crack/ like a stick in his throat."

"Waking, Working," which immediately precedes "Mister," opens

> I came to on the ground. In my fist
> a handful of indestructible earth.
> Already then there was this idea

> of work. The body moving like a scythe
> over its broad gold day.

We wake to work, to the ownership of our bodies by those for whom we labor. The following poem, "We Called Goodbye, but She Was Already Gone" ends with more plum imagery. In this case, the plums "she" loved are left to rot and the poem ends "Now she belongs to us/the way they/belong to the wind."

"Mister" is in *No Starling*'s first section, Doorman. Other poems in this section include "White Marginalia," eulogy for "a good girl. . . .her face and so many others/slide forth in dark drawers that clang/like coins in a tin box." In "Doorman" the character has an undertaker-like quality: "He wields/scalpels and chisels. He goes in and goes in." There are "New Boys" appearing in several poems, charged with the work of body disposal. The first poem in the section imagines a speaker "driving with the dead Nance/ in the truck bed." These may be read as imaginary aspects of the speaker, dreamscapes, and also reminders of our violence-strewn society, a fearful music we hear singing in the body.

Embodying universal ideas about work, fear, and uncertainty, these poems have a particular resonance in the current economic and political uncertainties. I hear an echo of GW Bush's "I am the decider" in the use of the word "bringer," and too often, like children, we look to our leaders to burn off the fogs of uncertainty. There is a particular tenderness and attention rightly paid to those for whom work is little more than a daily struggle to survive. But further and deeper, I relate to "Mister" as a poet and feel the writer laboring in and with (and against) form and forms, with the fearful masters in mind (here perhaps in echoes of Stevens, Frost, and Williams), with the uncertainty of outcomes, like an artisan, like someone in the middle of work who leaves off thinking to move and sing.

## About the Contributors

**Aaron Anstett**'s collections are *Sustenance, No Accident,* and *Each Place the Body's.* A chapbook, *The Next Thing You Know,* is forthcoming from Kattywompus Press. He lives in Colorado with his wife, Lesley, and children.

**Douglas Basford**'s poems, translations, and critical prose appear in *Ambit, Western Humanities Review, Poetry, Subtropics, Words without Borders, The FSG Book of Twentieth-Century Italian Poetry, JMWW, SubStance, Smartish Pace, The Hopkins Review,* and elsewhere. He teaches at SUNY-Buffalo, co-edits the online journal *Unsplendid,* and is the Reviews and Prose Editor for *The National Poetry Review.*

**Jaydn DeWald**, an MFA candidate at Pacific University, currently lives with his wife in San Francisco, CA, where he writes, plays bass for the DeWald/Taylor Quintet, and serves as an Associate Poetry Editor for *Silk Road.* His work has appeared or is forthcoming in *Bellevue Literary Review, Columbia Poetry Review, The Hollins Critic, West Branch, Witness,* and others.

**Alice B. Fogel**'s most recent book of poems, *Be That Empty,* was a national poetry bestseller in 2008, and in 2009 *Strange Terrain* (how not to "get" poetry) came out. She is a proof reader and copy editor, teaches writing and other arts, and also is an award-winning designer and creator of custom and refashioned clothing (www.lyriccouture.com).

**Dorine Jennette** is the author of *Urchin to Follow* (The National Poetry Review Press, 2010). Her poetry and prose have appeared in journals such as *Verse Daily, the Journal, Puerto del Sol, the New Orleans Review, the Los Angeles Review,* and *the Georgia Review.* Originally from Seattle, she earned her MFA at New Mexico State University and her PhD at the University of Georgia. She works in reference publishing, and is an editor of *the American Poetry Journal.* She lives in the Bay Area.

**Les Gottesman**'s poems have appeared in print and online journals and magazines including *Juked, FutureCycle, Anamesa, Beatitude, Harper's, Antioch Review,* and *Columbia Review.* Les has been a teacher in San Francisco for over 30 years. and received an MFA in Writing from California College of the Arts in 2011.

**Elizabeth Hughey** is the author of *Sunday Houses the Sunday House* (University of Iowa Press) and *Guest Host* (The National Poetry Review Press). She is a contributing editor at Bateau Press and a founder of the Desert Island Supply Co., a free creative writing center for kids in the Birmingham area. New poems can be found in *American Poetry Review, 27 rue de fleures* and the *White Whale Review,* and she just received an NEA fellowship.

**Gerry LaFemina**'s latest books are the full-length collection *Vanishing Horizon* (Anhinga Press, 2011) and a chapbook, *Steam Punk* (Small's Press, 2012). He directs the Frostburg Center for Creative Writing were he is an associate professor of English. He divides his time between Maryland and New York.

**Erika Lutzner** is the editor of *Scapegoat Review*. She curates Upstairs at Erika's, a monthly writer's salon in Williamsburg, Brooklyn. Her work can be found in various places such as *failbetter, Eclectica Magazine, wicked alice,* and *Tygerburning Journal.* Her first book, *Invisible Girls,* is available through Dancing Girl Press.

**Elizabeth McLagan'**s poems have appeared in *Poetry Northwest, American Literary Review, Beloit Poetry Journal, Third Coast, Iron Horse Literary Review, Bellingham Review, Southeast Review, Verse Daily* and elsewhere.  She was an AWP Intro Award winner in 2001, the 2006 recipient of the Frances Locke Memorial Award from Bitter Oleander, and the 49th Parallel Poetry Award winner from Bellingham Review in 2009. She teaches creative writing at Portland Community College. Her first book of poetry, *In the White Room,* is due out from CW Books in May 2013. Visit her at elizabethmclagan.com/

**Lynne Potts** lives in Boston and New York. Her work has appeared in *Paris Review, Denver Quarterly, California Quarterly, Meridian, Southern Humanities Review, Oxford Magazine, Southern Poetry Review, American Letters and Commentary, Hayden's River Review, Texas Review, Guernica, Cincinnati Review, SPEC, New American Writers, New Millennium Writing* and other literary journals. She won the *Backwards City Review* prize for poetry and the Bowery Poetry Club HD. She is Poetry Editor for *AGNI* at Boston University and former Poetry Editor of the *Columbia Journal of Art and Literature.*

**R. T. Smith** is Writer-in-Residence at Washington and Lee University, where he also edits *Shenandoah.*  His recent publications include Sherburne: Stories (Stephen F. Austin Univ. Press, 2011) and poems in *Sewanee Review, Pleiades, Five Points and Southern Humanities Review.*  He teaches on occasion in the Converse College MFA program and is twice winner of the Library of Virginia Poetry Book of the Year Award.  Smith lives in Rockbridge County, Virginia.

**Maggie Smith** is the author of *Lamp of the Body* (Red Hen Press), *Nesting Dolls* (Pudding House), and *The List of Dangers* (Kent State University Press). Her poems have appeared or are forthcoming in *The Southern Review, The Paris Review, Shenandoah, Diode, Indiana Review,* and elsewhere. She has recently received fellowships the Ohio Arts Council, the Virginia Center for the Creative Arts, and the National Endowment for the Arts. You can find her online at www.maggie-smithpoet.com.

**Tony Trigilio**'s newest book is the poetry collection *Historic Diary* (BlazeVOX, 2011).   He is a member of the core poetry faculty at Columbia College Chicago and co-edits *Court Green.*

**Emily Wolahan'**s poetry has been published in *Boston Review, elimae, DIAGRAM, New Linear Perspectives* and *Drunken Boat.*  A graduate of the Columbia University MFA program, she now lives in Newcastle upon Tyne, England, where she teaches poetry and edits *JERRY Magazine.*

www.alexandraeldridge.com

Alexandra Eldridge

*Imagination... the only real and eternal world.*

# The 2013 **APJ** Book Prize

2012 winner was **Richard Garcia's** *The Other Odyssey.*
2011 winner was **Dan Rosenberg's** *The Crushing Organ.*
2010 winner was **Quinn Latimer's** *Rumored Animals.*
2009 winner was **Mark Conway's** *Dreaming Man, Face Down.*
2008 winner was **Lisa Lewis's** *Burned House with Swimming Pool.*
2007 winner was **Matthew Guenettes's** *Sudden Anthem.*
The 2006 winner was **Theodore Worozbyt's** *The Dauber Wings.*

*Who will be the author of the next book in this series? You?*

The postmark deadline for entries to the 2012 *The American Poetry Journal* Book Prize is February 28, 2013. To enter, submit 50-65 paginated pages of poetry, table of contents, acknowledgments, bio, email address for results (No SASEs; manuscripts will be recycled), and a $27.00 non-refundable fee for each manuscript entered. The winner will receive $1000, publication, and 20 copies. All entries will be considered for publication. All styles are welcome. Multiple submissions are acceptable. Simultaneous submissions are acceptable, but if your manuscript is accepted for publication elsewhere you must notify The *American Poetry Journal* and/or Dream Horse Press immediately. Fees are non-refundable. Judging will be anonymous; writers' names should not appear anywhere on the manuscript. Please include your name and biographical information in a separate cover letter. Please be sure to include your email address. The winner is chosen by the editor of The *American Poetry Journal*, J.P. Dancing Bear. Close friends, students (former or present), and relatives of the the editor are NOT eligible for the contest; their entry fees will be refunded.

The *American Poetry Journal* Book Prize entries may be sent online (save paper/postage/money! - $25) or by sending an entry fee of $27 with manuscript to:

The *American Poetry Journal* book prize
P. O. Box 2080
Aptos, California 95001-2080
Make checks payable to: Dream Horse Press

**dreamhorsepress.com**

M. B. MCLATCHEY's poems have been published in journals such as *The American Poetry Journal, The National Poetry Review, Shenandoah,* and *The Southern Poetry Review*. Recent awards include the Annie Finch Poetry Award from the *National Poetry Review, The Spoon River Poetry Review*'s Editor's Prize, The Penelope Niven Award in Creative Nonfiction, the Vachel Lindsay Poetry Prize, and finalist for the May Swenson Book Award. She earned her graduate degree in Comparative Literature at Harvard University and the MFA from Goddard College. Currently, she is Assistant Professor of Humanities and Writing at Embry-Riddle University in Daytona Beach, Florida, where she lives with her husband, two sons, and a retired cat.

DAVID MOOLTEN is a physician specializing in transfusion medicine. He writes and practices in Philadelphia, Pennsylvania. His most recent book of verse, *Primitive Mood*, won the T.S. Eliot Prize from Truman State and was published in 2009.

ALAN JUDE MOORE was born in Dublin. He is the author of three collections of poetry, *Black State Cars* (Salmon Poetry, 2004), *Lost Republics* (Salmon Poetry, 2008) and *Strasbourg* (Salmon Poetry, 2010).

JOHN A. NIEVES has poems forthcoming or recently published in journals such as: *Beloit Poetry Journal, Crazyhorse, Southern Review, Hayden's Ferry Review, New York Quarterly, Ninth Letter* and *Cincinnati Review*. He won the 2011 Indiana Review Poetry Prize and the 2010 Southeast Review AWP Short Poetry contest. His work has also appeared on *Verse Daily*. He received his PhD from the University of Missouri in 2012.

DOUG RAMSPECK is the author of four poetry collections. His most recent book, *Mechanical Fireflies* (2011), received the Barrow Street Press Poetry Prize. His first book, *Black Tupelo Country* (2008), received the John Ciardi Prize for Poetry. His poems have appeared in journals that include *Slate, The Kenyon Review, The Southern Review, The Georgia Review, Alaska Quarterly Review, AGNI,* and *Prairie Schooner*. He teaches creative writing and directs the Writing Center at The Ohio State University at Lima.

LUCAS SCHEELK writes poetry and researches autistic discourse and queer discourse. He has performed in the 20% Theatre Company remount production of *The Naked I: Wide Open*. His writing has appeared in the *Lambda Literary Review*.

MARK SMITH-SOTO MFA is Professor of Spanish and editor of *International Poetry Review* at the University of North Carolina at Greensboro. He is the author of *Our Lives Are Rivers* (University Press of Florida, 2003), and *Any Second Now* (Main Street Rag Publishing Co., 2006). His poetry has appeared in *Antioch Review, Kenyon Review, Literary Review, Nimrod, The Sun* and many other publications. In 2010, Unicorn Press brought out his work of translation *Fever Season*, the selected poetry of Costa Rican writer Ana Istarú. His most recent works are *Berkeley Prelude: A Lyrical Memoir* (Unicorn Press, 2012) and the chapbook *Splices*, due out next year from Finishing Line Press.

ELIZABETH HARMON THREATT is currently a student at the University of Cincinnati where I am studying for my PhD in English and Creative Writing with an emphasis in poetry. She has had poems published in *The Rectangle, Cold Mountain Review, The Aurorean, Poet Lore, Big Muddy, Rattle, Mississippi Review,* and others.

JOSHUA WARE lives in Denver, CO. His first book, *Homage to Homage to Homage to Creeley*, (Furniture Press, 2011). Three of his chapbooks will be released in 2012: *Imaginary Portraits* (Greying Ghost Press); *How We Remake the World* (Slope Editions), co-written with Trey Moody; and *SDVIG* (alice blue books), co-written with Natasha Kessler. His writing and collages have appeared in *American Letters & Commentary, Colorado Review, Conduit, New American Writing, New Orleans Review, Third Coast, Quarterly West,* and *Western Humanities Review*.

# Contributors

**JENNIFER BOYDEN**'s is the author of two poetry collections, *The Mouths of Grazing Things*, winner of the Brittingham Prize in Poetry, and the forthcoming *The Declarable Future*, which was awarded the Four Lakes Prize in Poetry. As a recipient of the PEN Northwest Wilderness Writing Residency Award, Boyden lived and wrote for one year in a remote cabin in southern Oregon where she barred the doors against drunk bears and wielded a chainsaw out of necessity and satisfaction. She is currently in the startup phase of shaping a writing and arts residency program dedicated to collaboration and ecology on the Oregon coast.

**JAMES CIHLAR**'s reviews have appeared in the *Brooklyn Rail, Prairie Schooner, Western American Literature, Coldfront,* and the *Minneapolis Star Tribune*.

**CHRIS CRITTENDEN** has been widely published (one thing he is proud of is that his poems were featured on *The Portland Review*'s website for four months). His full-length collection Jugularity just came out from Stonesthrow, he is a teaching artist at the Poetry Coop, and he blogs as *Owl Who Laughs*. Living fifty miles from any traffic light, he writes next to a spruce forest and teaches ethics courses for the University of Maine at Machias.

**TAYLOR COLLIER** currently lives in Syracuse, NY. Work has appeared or is forthcoming in *DIAGRAM, the minnesota review, Southern Indiana Review, Yemassee* and others.

**LORRAINE DORAN**'s work can be found in *FIELD, Gulf Coast,* and *Barn Owl Review*.

**REBECCA FARIVAR** is the author of *Correct Animal* (Octopus Books, 2011) and chapbooks *Am Rhein* (Burnside Review, 2013) and *American Lit* (Dancing Girl Press, 2011). She holds an MFA from St. Mary's College of California and hosts the podcast *Break The Line*. Individual poems have been published or are forthcoming in *Denver Quarterly, The Volta, 6x6, Columbia Poetry Review, Word For/Word, RealPoetik,* and elsewhere. She lives in Oakland, California.

**PAUL HOSTOVSKY** is the author of four books of poetry, *Bending the Notes, Dear Truth, A Little in Love a Lot,* and *Hurt Into Beauty*. His poems have won a Pushcart Prize and two Best of the Net Awards. To read more of his work, visit him at www.paulhostovsky.com.

**JESSICA JEWELL** has work in *Nimrod, The Adirondack Review, Harpur Palate, Copper Nickel, Rhino, wicked alice, Poetry Midwest, Barn Owl Review, Poems & Plays, Angle Magazine,* among others. dancing girl press recently published her chapbook, *SLAP LEATHER*.

**RUSTIN LARSON**'s poetry has appeared in *The New Yorker, The Iowa Review, North American Review, Poetry East, Saranac Review, Poets/Artists* and other magazines. He is the author of *The Wine-Dark House* (Blue Light Press, 2009) and *Crazy Star* (selected for the Loess Hills Book's Poetry Series in 2005). He was a featured poet at the Poetry at Round Top Festival in May 2012.

**ÉIREANN LORSUNG** is the author of *Music for Landing Planes By* and Her Book, both from Milkweed Editions. She edits a journal, *1110*, and runs a poetry chapbook press, Miel.

**STEPHEN MASSIMILLA**'s latest book, *The Plague Doctor in His Hull-Shaped Hat*, is forthcoming as a contest winner from Stephen F. Austin State University Press. His collection *Forty Floors from Yesterday* won the Bordighera Prize, and *Almost a Second Thought* was runner-up for the Salmon Run National Poetry Book Award judged by X.J. Kennedy. Other awards include the Grolier Prize and a Van Renssalaer Award judged by Kenneth Koch. He holds an M.F.A. and Ph.D. from Columbia University and teaches at Columbia and the New School.

optician,/ who says the problem is all mine."

This thrust forward manifests itself to ideas of death. In "Soliloquy II" the speaker contemplates, "Perhaps I was mist in a previous life,/ maybe that's why I can't understand/ these instructions. Or perhaps I'll/ be, in my next life, mist."

The voice in these poems is constantly on verge of some dread or depression never announced. It remains beyond a wall, a wall the speaker knocks upon; an impression of what is beyond echoes through, but is never seen. In "Soliloquy, ii" she says "I'm scared of/ nothing. Depends how you define 'nothing'—/ I think it's the little shard of whatnot/ I keep trying to name." *Game of Boxes* is exactly about these unknowns in life— the unknowns of what it is to be.

The lover in "XXII" of "Sweet Double, Talk-Talk" says, "his face is a clue to me but I don't know/ what it means"; after ruminating on what is beyond death, the speaker in the third section says, " When did it/ get so mysterious?" These people keep moving onward into the blur of unknowns that perpetually unfurl before us. The children in "Chorus" intone, "Who knows why we are here, it's a 'mystery'./ We're getting older,/ and when no one is watching/ we climb right into it." Or another way of saying it is simply, "Carry on, carry on."

adulthood.

\*

The second section, "Of All Faces," is comprised of one long erotic poem in twenty-four parts called "Sweet Double, Talk-Talk." I would say these poems owe a slight nod to Adrienne Rich's "21 Love Poems" except Barnett's are marked with combat. Love—as they say—is a battle and these poems are fierce with opposition—between partners in the field of erotic love and its relation to an ideal of high-minded love. Where the self fits in the field creates a flux. There's anxiety, hesitation, and unconscious motivations. "I could tarry a man like him," Barnett says in XIX, the wordplay sexually dual-ing and dueling with "marry." Other oppositions and pairings arise.

> IV.
>
> I know agape means both dumbly
> open and love not the kind of love
> that climbed the stairs to you.

"Sweet Double, Talk-Talk" is full of aching eroticism and candid sex-talk where a lover's "voice fills my veins,// my mind, my restless/ anatomical// slit" and, "I'd never been so thirsty [..] I/ climbed the steps to my hurt on his// and his on mine./ We poured the hot drink."

In this section a narrative emerges in which the speaker shakily moves from apathy to ambivalence and finally connection with her sexual partner. The relationship of child/parent in the "Endless Forms Most Beautiful" is replaced by desire. Among other pillow-talk, the speaker says of her partner, "You say your mother's still here/ but I'm the woman in the bed" and later "he whispers *there, there* as if I were a child/ and not a woman lying beside him// but what's wrong with that."

\*

In the last of these three sections, "The Modern Period," the poet pushes beyond the domesticity of the first two. If cracks of anxiety and dread in the earlier sections led voices to seek comfort in relationships, now a more clinical method dominates. "In the Cabinet of What's Expired" she finds "Salves, creams, dreams in their shiny metal tins:/ the balm of yes/ is now the balm of no— // But it's a pretty silver hope,/ and I still swallow it— I let it wash down my throat." In a Rite-Aid, "the handsome new pharmacist [...] prescribes the moon,/ which has often helped before." Later, the speaker visits "The Beautiful Optician" to get replacement glasses. The subtextual play here is trying to find a way to fix the "eye" versus the "I." What problems are there with the "I?" "I don't always like what I see,/ I'm a little afraid [..] I tell none of this/ to the beautiful

The first section, "Endless Forms Most Beautiful," ricochets between the voices of mothers and children. Barnett's portrait of childhood does not delve into the clichés of an adult's meditations on innocence—a lost world of magic and skinned knees and joyful disregard for responsibility and society. Instead, the "chorus" of children find holes in the curtains adults place before their eyes and question the mystery of what it is to be older, what is beyond them, what is darker. "We want to know the reasons for everything/ but the mothers tell us *be patient*." It feels like the children are asking about capital-E Everything.

Catherine Barnett shows the wisdom of children is less in the ability to articulate their feelings, and more in their true perception of those feelings. In one of the many poems titled "Chorus," the collective voice of children sings:

> *What's wrong?* we ask.
> To keep from answering, they keep reading.
>
> *The Book of Illusions,*
> *The End of Illusions,*
>
> and *On Not Being Able to Sleep.*
> But we know more than they think.

Despite knowing more, the chorus is unable to specify what is the matter with the adults. There is always something beyond understanding, beyond language. Adults, too, confront this displacement in Barnett's poems. In "Categories of Understanding":

> I'm studying the unspoken.
> "What?" my son asks.
> "What are you looking at?"
> But there is no explaining,
> I can only speak the way the light
> falls, the way the cotton sheet
> lays itself over his sleeping or resting
> or dissolving body, touching him with
> its ephemera, its oblivion.

It's in this gap-space the first-section of poems exist— a child's attempt at comprehending the larger world and putting these feelings into words. "Dreamlike" will be used by some to describe the logic here, but it will be a misnomer. These sparse, controlled poems fit into the slim, liminal space between wake and sleep, between feelings and speech, between childhood and

> grief of your death is the shriek shriek shrieking
> hare in the words, solitary pulse that inks in
> the absolute darkness from my pen to my pain pain painful
> wheel steering, world stopping, time spotting, breath-stop.

González's unblinking look at mortality naturally summons a complementary awareness of eternity. In the second section of numbered flower poems, "Floriocho" hints at a knowledge that lives in the X chromosome, thus extending life beyond birth and death dates: "your grandmother knew before marriage // that her husband would outlive her by twenty-four years. Vision in fever / during adolescent menstruation. . . . / she sensed one of her sons would chromosome / a girl." The last section of the book focuses on the women surrounding a character from González's family lore, the Mortician who threw a monthly party in the funeral home, in effect for his future clients.

Erudite, provocative, and poignant, *Black Blossoms* is a far-reaching exploration of women's images in art. Amidst bleak grotesqueries, Gonzalez injects dark humor, as in "The Ballad of Lucila la Luciérnaga." This daring persona poem uses the film noir trope of a narrator who speaks from the dead, as this circus performer who died when her caravan plunged into a ravine describes how she acquired her nickname: "My lover called me firefly by the way my buttocks / lit up at the height of excitement as he took me from behind. // I wore a skirt with lights after that . . ." If comedy rarely gets the upper hand over tragedy in *Black Blossoms*, this omnibus meditation on death, gender, and art is testament to the versatility and fearlessness of one our most prolific and generous authors.

# THE GAME OF BOXES
by Catherine Barnett, Graywolf Press, 2012
80 pages. $15. Paperback
ISBN-13: 978-155597-620-0

### REVIEWED BY SAM WOODWORTH

"Carry on, carry on—," the final phrase in the first section of Catherine Barnett's *The Game of Boxes*, coincidentally happens to be the first phrase on M-83's *Hurry Up, We're Dreaming*, a sprawling double-LP concerned with how we make meaning as we mature. If the zeitgeist managed to bring me two thematically similar works across genres at the same time, the lush orchestration of the music contrasts with the quietness of the poems. Barnett's big questions happen in small places: the gaps in understanding between mothers and a "chorus" of children, the anxiety of erotic love, and a voice that pushes out of these boundaries and into a public space.

offers a comprehensive critique of women's physical suffering as sources of aesthetic and spiritual enlightenment.

Inspired by German painter Otto Dix's painting of Anita Berber, a nude dancer popular in the Weimar era, wearing a brilliant red dress, González's opening poem observes the habitual manner in which political movements stake claims on women's rights as a means of advancing their own fortunes:

> War as Woman is what it should be called,
>     this dress stretched open like a battlefield,
>         this arsenal of fingertips and bullet kiss,
> this bloody bed with a skull rising through it.

If the female body itself was a battlefield in which the repressive forces of rising Nazi power silenced the artistic experimentation of German Expressionism, we have seen similar attempts to politicize the ownership of women's bodies since.

Throughout *Black Blossoms*, González pushes the envelope, delving into disturbing imagery while maintaining poetic balance. He sees Dix's choice to paint Berber clothed as meta-nakedness, equating it to the essence under the skin: "this devil that slipped / out of every dress except for the one / that coated her skin after her body sliced open." Dedicating this poem to Marion Ettlinger, who has photographed such authors as Truman Capote, Alice Munro, and Cormac McCarthy (as well as providing the author photo for this book), González honors Anita Berber the dancer, the woman as artist rather than subject, as he finds echoes of her creativity surviving in the artifact of this portrait.

Images of physical decay abound in this book full of dismembered limbs and resolute morbidity. The title poem takes as inspiration Francisco Goya's fourteen "Black Paintings," notably the graphic *Saturn Eating His Son*, in which the god holds a headless corpse. "Mise-en-Scene" turns the tables on the familiar story of Lizzie Borden, suggesting motivation for a daughter's patricide: "You buried your father the night / he wanted to step inside you the way he enters the house." In "Dead Woman's Jewelry at an Estate Sale," a New York shopper imagines the life of the deceased woman whose possessions she surveys on display, leading to one of the book's few consolatory images of death: "This is where/ a collector of bright things belongs, sunning her entire /grave above ground." After purchasing a pair of earrings, Mrs. Drummond fancies the husband's ghost whispers in her ear, while she considers that through the contemplation of artifacts she has extended the owner's existence, just as someone will do the same for her after her death.

"Vespertine" is dedicated to Roxanna Rivera, as is the book: "in loving memory of my poet-girl." As González has explained, she was a young, talented writer who died in an auto accident in 2003 after the poet had encouraged her parents to let her leave home in California to study with him in college. This directly personal implication explains the note of inconsolable loss that dominates the book:

Transdyke Sisters" is brilliant because it offers a safe space within text.

    Kaveney also unapologetically reminds the reader of the important place that transgender people, specifically transwomen, hold in the GLBT movement in her poem "Stonewall," referencing the protests and riots against the police raids at New York's Stonewall Inn on June 28, 1969. Kaveney points out that transwomen (especially transwomen of color) were substantially responsible for the demonstration that ended up becoming the start of the modern GLBT rights movement. I highly recommend this poem for historical reference, and because it's one of the more powerful pieces of the book.

> The riot was the bar
> and
> the riot was the street.
> The street where people lived.
> The street where people walked,
> Too young, too queer, too poor, too brown.

Readers familiar with Roz Kaveney will recognize the poem "Shot, Stabbed, Choked, Strangled, Broken: a ritual for November 20th" that previously appeared in Kate Bornstein's *Gender Outlaws: The Next Generation*. As we observe Transgender Day of Remembrance every November, Kaveney's poem reminds us of the terrible loss of so many of our trans* brothers and sisters every year due to other people's transphobia and violence: "Their stories are remembered by us, on this day and always."

    *Dialectic of the Flesh* is like taking a ride back in time through the emotionally powerful moments of someone else's life. Roz Kaveney's poetry tears at the heartstrings, compelling us to invest in her words from the first page to the last.

# BLACK BLOSSOMS
by Rigoberto González, Fourway Books, 2011
76 pages. $15.95. Paperback
ISBN-13: 978-1-93556-15-4

### REVIEWED BY JAMES CIHLAR

Rigoberto González is the author of eight books of poetry and prose, a regular book reviewer for the *El Paso Times*, and an associate professor at Rutgers. In his stunning, lush, and disturbing collection *Black Blossoms*, he examines the historical depiction of women in art. From Lizzie Borden to the Grimms' "The Girl without Hands," from Frida Kahlo to Francisco Goya, the poet builds a convincing case of cultural obsession with female dismemberment, decay, and mortality. Deploying ekphrasis, allusion, and dramatic monologue, time, a mother tongue, a second language, a body, bodies, a landscape, a sense of smell, a memory linked to all these things, a blood stocked with shared cells. As Erdrich writes in "Rich Hour," "it is clear I have always been here, in this courtyard, with these starlings."

# Dialectic of the Flesh
by Roz Kaveney, A Midsummer Night's Press, 2012
64 pages. $14.95. Paperback
ISBN-10: 1938334000
ISBN-13: 978-1-938334-00-9

## Reviewed by Lucas Scheelk

It's a rare experience to read a modern poetry book that structures a good portion of its poems in a Shakespearian sonnet format. This caught me by surprise as I read Roz Kaveney's *Dialectic of the Flesh*. Her sonnets are appealing because they are an homage to the language of romance. The subject of the sonnets isn't obvious. Are they addressed to a lover? To the poet? To her transition? As the book intensifies to the very last page, readers may continue to wonder. I personally went back and forth between multiple possibilities before I found myself not worrying so much about the "right" answer. The openness of Kaveney's poetry could be easily allow more than one response, which is a strength of the book.

In addition to romance, *Dialectic of the Flesh* touches on such themes as religion ("Loving Despair"), transitioning ("Cunt," "Valediction"), and transgender life ("For My Transdyke Sisters," "Transition"). Kaveney does not hesitate disclosing that she is a transwoman, although she points out, especially in "For My Transdyke Sisters," that such disclosure must be taken seriously.

> Some of us love our sisters. On a date
> saves time, we can avoid the big reveal.
> They told us we were sick. Here's how we heal,
> here's how those storms of self-contempt abate.

The poem provides social commentary about "the big reveal," regarding the disclosure of trans* status, and the effects and repercussions it has on the lives those of transwomen who disclose. While I know a little of what it's like (I'm a transman, myself), there are other experiences about disclosing that I could not know firsthand. This poem is written for transwomen, and assumes their familiarity with the subject matter, thus building community. The poet does not feel like she has to explain these experiences to them, as she might for readers who are cisgender, or who have a different trans* status. "For My

The cells in Erdrich's poems are by no means all bodily: there are, of course, literal human cells (which appear throughout the book like a thread of evidence linking newer poems to older ones), but there are also rich possibilities for the reading of the cell as metaphor in this book. Cell—as quickly as the human comes to mind, so does the human mode of punishment. And it's not an immense jump from the jail cell to the reservation, from a state penitentiary to economic, social, and political conditions which make movement impossible, which make a landscape like a cell, a place it's difficult or impossible to leave by choice. Poems like "Butter Maiden and Maize Girl Survive Death Leap" and "Two Sides" (which appears twice in the book—once in a lineated form, and once in prose) point to a violence and containment which extends beyond the physical. Movement is not impossible, in these poems; people do leave. But the fact of systematic historical and contemporary violence against Native people in the US informs the figures and the stories that appear here.

In their deftest moments, Erdrich's poems unite these facts—the fact of violence and the fact of possibility. "Black and White Monument, Photo circa 1977" is one poem that does so. It echoes cellular images in other poems by its form (three sections), its prompting subject (ostensibly a photograph), and by the way each section hedges in a memory and a way of dealing with the information contained in the photograph. As a whole, the poem also acknowledges that the single space—the cell, the photograph—alone is not enough. The girls in the photograph and the barely remembered cousins whose babies they hold have different stories, only parts of which can be contained in this single moment. While there is meaning there, or information, it is also true that "we always know more or less than what a photo can show". There will always be something escaping, left out, known differently, misremembered. The story, the container, the inefficiency of language will always be incomplete; through the small holes, other possibilities for the story leak out, grow.

The strongest poems in *Cell Traffic* are poems about mixedness, chimera; they are places where, as Erdrich writes, "your cells and hers/ flowed back and forth", places of interchange. They are often sly and smart—wonderful qualities—as in many of the poems from *National Monuments*. They allow for the presence of what is not known, for mystery, as in "The Shapes We Make":

> Letters, yes, printing some sentiment. Spelling it out together. Bent this way, curved that way. O we make and H. Hand in hand. H. You raise your arms, an X of joy. O we two and H. Hand in hand. H.

where mystery—the H-ness of H, the O-ness of O—is playful, too, and deep. *Cell Traffic* is a rangy collection. Parts of the book are uneven; when the poet writes about learning (and when she writes "keep revising, poetry students!" in the notes), her own awareness of writing as an ongoing process, one that takes place in time and space, is tangible. Later, more subtle and accomplished poems couple with early ones and in doing so demonstrate a sense of being-descended. The poems do not come from nowhere. They come from a place, a

# Cell Traffic: New and Selected Poems
by Heid E. Erdrich, University of Arizona Press, 2012
272 pages, paperback, $19.95
ISBN-10: 0816530084
ISBN-13: 978-0816530083

### Reviewed by Éireann Lorsung

Heid Erdrich's *Cell Traffic*, which collects work from Erdrich's three books along with new and previously unpublished work, establishes from the start a concern with inside, outside, and movement between these two spaces. Beginning with the title, and echoed throughout the book's ten sections, we are given the figure of a cell as a way to understand relation. The cell, which is unitary, is also osmotic, able to absorb. It is also able to be absorbed.

But even the absorbed cell, we learn in poems such as "Microchimerism" and "Blood Chimera," can retain some trace of the other. The echo of the ancestral—of the mother—lives on in the bodies of her daughters and granddaughters. Here too are the echo of poetic ancestors, with whose words Erdrich playfully engages, in poems such as "Some Elsie" and "The Theft Outright." But the play is serious: in addressing work by canonical poets like Williams and Frost, Erdrich not only sets herself among them (I, too, sing America!) but sets up a critique of their work on their own ground. Playfulness is a tone and a tactic, not a way of escaping from responsibility. While Erdrich calls others to responsibility in these poems and in others ("Guidelines for the Treatment of Sacred Objects," for example) she also acknowledges that no writer writes alone, "but by a grace,/a blue silk threads our words/makes our work both ancestor and elder,/descended of one through the other/.../My words are not my own." Her debts—to mother, sisters, children; to translator and language teacher and "Young Poets with Roman Noses"—tie her to the people and places of her past and present.

There is a strong sense of cyclical recurrence throughout *Cell Traffic*: a rabbit eating berry canes seasonally; formal repetitions in the lovely "Red Vines: Lines for Deloria," which also has the doubling of chokecherry taste and the taste of a familiar candy; DNA throughout (and mothers, sisters, daughters, blood, and birth). The poem "Wearing Indian Jewelry" uses repeated phrases to underscore the dailiness of prayer: "*Every day, because these things/ are sacred, these things are prayer,*" Erdrich writes, ending the poem "every day every day every day." In the section of uncollected work, Erdrich's poems entwine with their translations into Ojibwe, repeating inexactly, as a feature might imprint from parent to child (or aunt to niece), for us later to say—*oh! Now I see how you are related!* Here we see the literary chimera, the trace of one way of saying something in another way of saying it.

Thus in part the traffic which forms the other half of the title ('cell traffic' refers to the movement of cells between a mother and her children in utero). As much as Erdrich's poems are about exploring ideas of what can live inside the confined space of a cell, they are also about what can depass its borders, or how indeed a cell, or the space a cell represents, can travel.

**M. B. McLatchey**
*Winner of the 2011 American Poet Prize*

# 1-800-THE-LOST

The weight of the receiver in my hand:
the down bird in my palm first lifting you.
The counselor's words: rehearsed, a burlesque bland.

The shift in time, the shift to looking through
her lens: today you are just one of two
hundred lost. My eyes fix on our bright fence.

I say your name, but you are no one new –
caught in an ancient book that she'll condense.
I want her to discuss you in the present tense.

I want the gods to stop pretending love
calls the departed home. We called you
with our various loves, had hope, hovered

over still fields; made wind like the gods do
before they come unhinged, let their rage loose
on an unresponsive yield. Fields gone deaf

and dumb; unshaken, fruitless ground, unmoved
by a neighborhood of mothers who left
their own to find you – tables, like mine, set.

I want the gods to swallow their prayers
whole. Choke up my child like the Olympians –
a girl, unbruised by her journey down their

throats. I want her at my table: fruit, alms
that the gods, I see, can give or take – balm
for the irritations I caused, or they

caused; gifts between us or perhaps among
themselves – a girl that they'll barter away.
I'm here. And I'm willing to talk, or trade.

JENNIFER BOYDEN
# Bad Advice

The empty cage could mean the rabbit
is near, or that there is no rabbit.

If the rabbit is near, fence the lettuce, get
the camera, tether the dogs, gather the neighbors,
beat the weeds, post a reward.

If no rabbit, options are limited: buy a rabbit;
make a rabbit from chicken wire and leaves;
burn the cage.

Most people prefer the rabbit,
even if it is missing.

The rabbit prefers the rabbit.
No rabbit prefers no rabbit. Few people
who do not see a rabbit think to prefer

no rabbit. This is why
the empty cage turns out to be necessary.
This is why it is poor advice to burn the cage.

Jennifer Boyden

## As If I Hadn't Worn It Quite Enough, Time Tattoos My Arms and Face

The lung is one way to enter a tree:
exhale, and breath makes a shadow;
the tree breathes back a dress of vapor.
It is not necessary to wear so much more
than that. Not when the body prints
its headline of loneliness on the bed:
Something Broke Here.
Exposure is made of light.
A filigree lace that hangs to dry on the air,
my breathing was meant to offset
the world pressing itself all over everything—
a little lingerie between what I hoped for
and the rest of it: machines, cowboys, hospital
breakage, motels, bags tossed from the car,
loose hands that confirm the cross references
of someone else's desire. What am I
if not a portrait of inhabitation? My body
assembles in the light: pinhole, curtain slit, keyshaft
of the onlooking. It takes so little to be inhabited.
Exposure, and each cell surges to what called forth
our first eyes, the first blooming of peonies
and foxgloves, the fanning-open of leaves,
which I hear and answer in breath.
I have not asked for more than my share.
I want to be answered when I ask, which means
to be dressed by breath, assembled
by light, and admitted into the history of trees.

Mark Smith-Soto
## Human, Unguarded

What an open face that person has, pale,
slender, dark rimmed glasses almost on the tip
of the nose, smile like a splice of light, long
eyes, mild tilt of the head, conversing with an
excited friend—Who's to tell, seated a little
too far away in this noisy place, if I'm looking
at a woman here or a young man, can't quite
catch the voice, the gender shifts gently one
to the other as the body in question sways,
bamboo in the wind, toward and away from me,
easy and unafraid. Why *unafraid*? I won't say
I understand it, the faint alarm that I feel spring
in my chest watching the figure turn and wave
and disappear out the door into the unbound day.

# Staring at the Blind

My eyes are the flies.
Your eyes are the spilled
milk. You are the cow
whose tail the farmer cut off—
defenseless now against the flies
which keep returning to feed
on the spilled white milk
of your eyes. "Let us pray,"
says the amazingly graceless
born-again Christian sitting
next to you on the subway train.
"Let us ask God, together, to restore
the sight to your eyes." Your eyes
are the guinea pigs. This guy is
a pig farmer from hell, trying
to cross-breed his faith with
your life story. I want to
cut his praying hands off.
I want to open his eyes to
your eyes. Your eyes are the bees
hovering, juking, making
something perfectly rich
and amazing on the inside,
something heavy and thick with
mystery, which some meddling hands
would unburden the bees of.
But the bees need no unburdening.

## Paul Hostovsky
# Half Moon

The two chairs
that we sat in

this morning
in our pajamas

in the sunny
kitchen

kissing

are still in the same
position

this evening
when I get home

in the dark
I sit in

one
then the other

Rustin Larson

# The Philosopher Savant Again Dreams of War

Insurgencies on boundaries of garden

Where chives are sacrificed, daylily, blue

Blow-balls, a war, quietly worked, Eden.

Paint pictures, peaceful, full of flowers, true.

I can't tell if I shall. A red bloom. A bloom.

The important thing to remember is

The subject is rather summery. You

Can see that, expendable into wakefulness.

Into the throat of the wolf fall deeper.

As you draw closer, be repelled, draw

The grotesque imitating some pasture

And think it beautiful. If you saw

The hundreds scythed in fields... and just suppose

Your impression is there and juxtaposed.

## Rustin Larson
# The Philosopher Savant Dreams of War

Back toward heaven, stalling, soon the birds

Chased each other overhead, circling, diving,

Silent in storms of white, silver, two birds.

Devoid of hue, the garden flowers swaying,

Last night, I dreamed a silent movie: "Wings."

Like lilac sprigs thrown in a mouth of earth

I cannot say this garden's not a thing,

A column of soldier's mown in death,

The garden death grows, the geography

Of close-cropped red. I hold the back of my head.

Without this art, there is no history;

From body bag a foot swings dead.

I click off the Nightly News.

But behold now the lilac that blooms.

## Taksim

the shields are melting into your walls Istanbul
the invasion is thousands of tiny parachute toys
fired into the air by illegal street traders
girls weave torn corners of canopies and veils
into the sky sky of gulls occupied by turbulence
water and light moving through the cistern
ghosts struggle for space on the square flags wave
flags always will voices mark the boundaries
of the city voices hearts and outstretched arms
Istanbul the shields are melting into your walls
the invasion is thousands of tiny parachutes

Jessica Jewell

## Sisi, Queen Of Hungary, on the Bank of Würmsee

I buoy into the water one skin
lighter than the blue color of night.
A yellow bird sleeps on the edge
of the driftwood. Under the moon
it takes the shape of a closed lily.
The wind and the sound of it
passes the bald cherry trees.
Joyful and young, I recall the smell
of the zither strings and its wood
on my father's fingers. His hair
is full of the sun's orange feathers.

Before the night they found Ludwig
floating dead, elbows lodged deep
into the shore mud, my father was more
or less a happy man, the type to believe
in happiness. Had happiness worked,
or love, I would still be here, my first
home, floating on its surface like ribbon.

she sat next to a man I swear
was Henry Winkler his right hand inching

behind her on the bench like a wet
worm I hate parties I pretend I'm in a children's story
any door

might lead to paradise
if opened in the proper spirit

I pretend I'm the last man in a world
populated by gorgeous robots I pretend
Nurse Anne will live forever

## Mark Neely
# Night Birds Plumbed the Aspen Grove

night birds plumbed the aspen grove
below a deck of desperate smokers all the houses
of the valley gave off tiny suns

I don't know what to do at parties
I pretend I'm Daryl Strawberry

that night I wore a pale suit
yellow tie and sandals to satisfy
Nurse Anne's foot fetish

the first of three wishes I was to grant her
my wishes weren't much better

modest fame
ten years for a dying father
and a sexual fantasy I can't disclose

a hidden spotlight fell from a barn-
high ceiling on the sheer bright

dresses of two women dancing I wondered
what was behind a few tightly shut doors I'm terrible
at parties I pretend I'm Sherlock Holmes

Behind the black door I heard my father snoring
we are all sick of mystery the sexual fantasy
involved the redhead dancer

fifty feet of rope
and an excitable chimpanzee

I never know what to do
in bed I do what Nurse Anne says
until I'm gasping

## Nightsong

A stump like a first-shaven boy.
Cloudbursts on clay fill the tenor ruts
riddling into gullies, nudge the throaty
whippoorwill by the clapboard –
ancient, pillowed window.

The man sleeps through untroubled dark.
She wakes to the familiar sound
of knees cracking in the night.

David Moolten
# Lullaby

An emancipated minor with a rose
In the teeth of a skull short shorts reveal
Branded on one thigh is still a girl,
Maybe more so in the way crushing flowers
Expresses their scent. She texts madly
Alongside the other colorful victims,
Loafers and failures, a choir of loud banter
Spiced with an infant's wailing she can flout
No longer. It's the usual Boschian hell
In DPW's take a number
Lobby of mercy where nothing strains belief
Except maybe the music leaving her mouth
As she clumsily hoists her offspring
Like a loaf of bread. It's not Brahms she hums
In her ZZ Top T-shirt and the key
Of tearing metal, and beyond the smirks
This priceless moment provides at her expense
Lies a child events must rub the wrong way
Into one raw blister. But for now, it's she
Who's exposed, oozing something like light
Around a medieval Madonna, the child
Wilting its head, ignorant as the rest,
Who don't crave beauty, only tenderness.

## Westman Island

I'm on my back in a field
hunting puffins.
Let me be clear:
this is not a dream.
I wait for them to fly
into shore. A fish
in the mouth
and they're safe.
Here comes
one with nothing.
I have a net.
Everyone wants
to make a mark
when they're new
and it's annoying
to us who are not new.
No one has found
a better way
to hunt puffins.
I catch the emptybeaked
one,
break his neck
on my leg.
I could lie here all day.

Joshua Ware

## "THE CELESTIAL ENNUI OF APARTMENTS"
*-after Wallace Stevens' "Notes Toward a Supreme Fiction"*

From Provence, there are cicadas
filled with flavor and caged in green. There is lavender
distilled into flacons. From an ex-lover
there is a floral robe cut
from out-dated fabric. There are songs
from Keats, our *watcher of the skies*; there are songs
from Shelley. *As a new planet swims* into this urban flat,
you read me *Adonais* and bathe my feet
in tepid water. Yes, death *tramples [us] into fragments*;
but the white cat eats canned tuna
in the corner, and your body beautiful in mirrors
walks naked across hardwood floors. We smoke
hash and watch classic American movies. Whether the realness
of the sun, or something duller from above, shines down
on us, I will shape these fragments into fictions
that know not grace and charm, but our love
ethereal, poetic, and surrounded
by cardboard boxes filled with books.

## Whisked Leaves

a brouhaha
of rucked galaxies

bursts into jugglers
with moods for pins,

then a lion's mane
dissolving a hind,

last kicks of her feet.

wind shivers
and the beasts erupt,

glib breaths
of a codgery volcano,

lava blustery,
dancing into lust,

roan harebells
and skittish bees,

who flit amber and orange,
fragile yet fast,

pollinating
to tremble and dip,

suddenly still
as if grained illusion,

sawdust on a stage.

Chris Crittenden
## Not So Vacant Lot

ants stream from a nipple,
blur of apricot roan.

no psalm binds them,
no sergeant-at-arms yells stop.

they scatter like drams
of fiery milk, curdling

as they go, gnashing emeralds
that skew in their mandibles,

and hounding nature
with snicks of flame.

a slyphid trips, blunders,
gets torn to gobbets,

each the size of a
matchstick head. the ants

ply their conga all day,
milling in droves, whirlpooling

to stuff their spoils
back down, into the adored

breast.

STEPHEN MASSIMILLA

# At Edge of Earth, Vacating on the Cheap

What comes next? A sky
so buzzard-lonely,
so severe.
Nothing less
than nothing whistling

through the teeth.
Rust of beaches,
mist of vines. Yellowlegs
swizzling S's in air-thin sheets
of surf. Ice-colored lizard
is a tiny lip twisting beneath
a cyclamen umbrella.

Faint snake of freight train
in the gaps
between canines of cliff,
rotted tree-stumps lisping: pistil, tower, quarter-
moon of dome. Past pure teeth of foam, raw lips

of sky: teach me to keep going
nowhere. Please, I have not come
from nowhere just to learn
how not to be scared. There is an end
to never settling for the reaches

of this earth, this dream of a precinct
no one can name. With stone eyes that take everything
for granted by blue hunger
that eats at this last spit of cloud-rock
overhead—I want to say (but won't) how far
I had to go to get
this far.

## Taylor Collier
# Yes

I'm on the phone with crazy and all I can say is yes
the company offered me three thousand dollars to quit
after training because they knew I'd defend my choice
to stay like a mother feels obligated to defend her idiot
son and we all know ugly is as ugly does and cherry butter
and grape jam make me selfish the other day I was sitting
at the bus station next to accountability who told me
about how all police officers are executioners or wait
maybe it was the other way around somehow there are
grackles all over the house and their screeching
and cackling rattles through the chimney's emptiness
like teeth crunching down on the fortune-cookie's missing
yes I know that everything that follows is in my likeness
yes maybe there should be a giant pit in the ground
where we dump all those that drop dead and yes I say
when she tells me about how all the men in the world
don't listen and yes I say when she claims all the trees
in upstate are being cleared and yes I say when she
complains of the raccoon in the garbage what else
can I say but yes there's no one to walk with tonight
no one to stroll the shore with when there is no shore
just the circumstance where I am the bed I sleep in
I am the pit of despair to which I wake each morning
I am the wind yes I am the sound in a shell yes I am
selfish yes I am accountable yes I am I am yes yes I am

Is this what it means to be forgotten? To want
your forgetfulness to follow the jagged line

of frozen creek, the body opening like a mouth
of moon, opening to the deep back

of the throat where the larynx trembles. To imagine
stepping into the prairie sea where mud is moored

as still as decades, where spores of snow cover
everything. To speak to the dead beneath the arms

of a shagbark hickory—stripped down to a bare
trunk—this tree that stands upright like a man.

## Doug Ramspeck
# The Dead in Their Forgotten Fields

You want to love them waiting in their cemetery,
waiting patient beyond the fence where snow is falling

pregnant to the earth, naked and vulnerable. Where last
summer, beyond the fence, the scrub of ankle

grass burned in August, and shadows in the field
made of sunlight an ancient skin of ground. Mud light.

Or maybe the shadow of a crow flew across the ground—
and disappeared. This bird that was incorporeal. Watch how

it moved as a spirit across the catbriers, the moccasin
flowers. The way a dream drifts past then is gone.

Or then a brown snake with its dark blotches
muscled through the goat's rue. The long ships of weeds

in their sea of vanishing. The heat pulling and tugging
at its rope where blackjack oaks flamed. Or later a pale

wound of moon like a great bird tearing at the sky's flesh,
the yellow weeds in a state of dishabille, femoral

morning returning suddenly to bleed in the crooked
stream no wider than an arm. But now, in winter,

we want this field to remember our bodies, to be
alert to the crows calling their auguries

from the trees, calling beneath clouds perfecting
their gray drifting, this slowness of passage.

## Promenade

Over the sound of invisible cars
a woman whispered, you are comforting
because you are dirty. She promised

she had only felt this way
about one other river. Also dirty.
Also thoughtfully named

with a flawed sense of direction
in mind. For the third time
I said the prayer I use

when something proves the world
exists. Once for a man wiring fixtures
for stars. Once before the bodies

began to pile up. Blessed is the sick day.
Blessed are things that open
for no reason. Instead of fireworks

the air of geraniums. Neighbors
walking home to another light
to hunch over. Blessed is the strange

backyard that dwarfs us, the shoemaker
who tut-tuts our bitten heels.
Tomorrow I will suddenly think

of windowboxes and not know why.
Her dress was the shape of crickets. It said
I am the perfect shade of green.

**Lorraine Doran**

# Postcard

(Tyniec)

You said be sure to see the cows, and I saw the cows. They were not like ours. There was no tether, no bell. There were six of them, gathered in a sparsely flowered field. You can tell they remember winter. They are not sentimental. Perhaps that is what makes us American. If you come this way, bring small change. You will hear the cows before you see them. It is cool in the monastery where they chant the mass in Latin. I know now why we are the way we are. It came to me as I watched them, nudging each other at the trough they shared.

# Autumnal

October happens this way—
a quick heat fools the bottom
leaves greener while the top
leaves are already wreathed
in old fire.

On the sidewalk, the crowd
is jacketed, or not jacketed, either
whispering jokes or prayers.

There are no clouds, but
something about the sky
implies rain.

The papers fill with ads
for masks, people
with the urge to hide
in plain sight.

Crows become buzzards.
Slats disappear from ancient
fences. Memories dial old
numbers, find them disconnected,
call back anyway.

Somewhere just above
the horizon, the day moon
realizes it is naked, but
not dreaming.

A squirrel plants a tree
no one will hang from
but all the doors that promise
something sweet are still closed.

## Reviews

**ÉIREANN LORSUNG**
 on *Cell Traffic: New and Selected Poems* by Heid E. Erdrich   **32**

**LUCAS SCHEELK**
 on *Dialectic of the Flesh* by Roz Kaveney   **34**

**JAMES CIHLAR**
 on *Black Blossoms* by Rigoberto González   **35**

**SAM WOODWORTH**
 on *The Game of Boxes* by Catherine Barnett   **37**

## CONTRIBUTORS   40

## Table of Contents

### Poetry

*John Nieves*
- Autumnal — 7

*Lorraine Doran*
- Postcard — 8
- Promenade — 9

*Doug Ramspeck*
- The Dead in Their Forgotten Fields — 10

*Taylor Collier*
- Yes — 12

*Stephen Massimilla*
- At Edge of Earth, Vacating on the Cheap — 13

*Chris Crittenden*
- Not So Vacant Lot — 14
- Whisked Leaves — 15

*Joshua Ware*
- "The Celestial Ennui of Apartments" — 16

*Rebecca Farivar*
- Westman Island — 17

*David Moolten*
- Lullaby — 18

*Mark Neely*
- Night Birds Plumbed the Aspen Grove — 19

*Elizabeth Harmon Threatt*
- Nightsong — 20

*Jessica Jewell*
- Sisi, Queen Of Hungary, on the Bank of Würmsee — 22

*Alan Jude Moore*
- Taksim — 23

*Rustin Larson*
- The Philosopher Savant Dreams of War — 24
- The Philosopher Savant Again Dreams of War — 25

*Paul Hostovsky*
- Half Moon — 26
- Staring at the Blind — 27

*Mark Smith-Soto*
- Human, Unguarded — 28

*Jennifer Boyden*
- As If I Hadn't Worn It Quite Enough, Time Tattoos My Arms and Face — 29
- Bad Advice — 30

*M. B. McLatchey*
- 1-800-THE-LOST — 31

**Sr. Editor:**
J.P. Dancing Bear

**Reviews Editor:**
James Cihlar

**Editor:**
Dorine Jennette

**Advisory Board:**
Jennifer Michael Hecht
Bob Hicok
Jane Hirshfield
C. J. Sage
Diane Thiel

**Subscriptions:**
Individuals: $15.00 per year
Institutions: $20.00 per year
(Please add $6.00 postage per year for subscriptions outside the United States.)

Web site: www.americanpoetryjournal.com

**The APJ reads magazine submissions online only.
Please see website for the latest guidelines.**

Address submissions, queries, orders, and all other correspondence to:

J.P. Dancing Bear, Editor
The American Poetry Journal
Post Office Box 2080
Aptos, California 95001-2080

The American Poetry Journal Copyright 2012 All Rights
Reserved
ISSN 1547-6650
ISBN 978-1-935716-22-8

Cover art: "Who Lit This Flame in Us" courtesy of Alexandra Eldridge
http://alexandraeldridge.com

The American Poetry Journal is a production of Dream Horse Press LLC

# The American Poetry Journal

# APJ

Issue number Twelve

www.ingramcontent.com/pod-product-compliance
Lightning Source LLC
Chambersburg PA
CBHW020947090426
42736CB00010B/1306